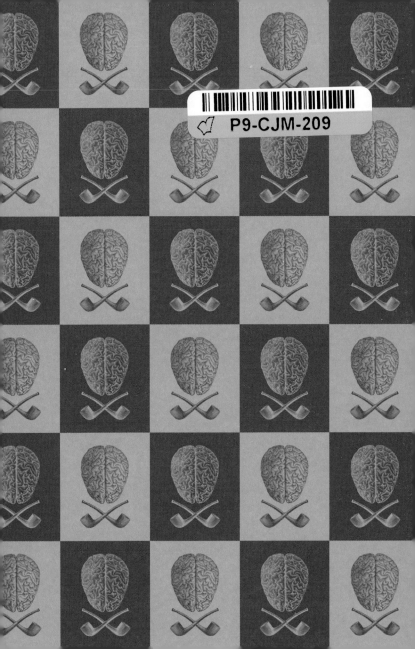

P9-CJM-209

In PRAISE of IDLENESS

A TIMELESS ESSAY

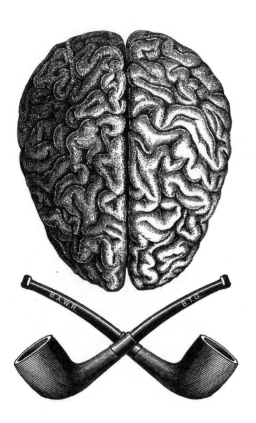

In PRAISE of IDLENESS

A TIMELESS ESSAY BY
BERTRAND RUSSELL
WINNER OF THE NOBEL PRIZE IN LITERATURE

WITH AN INTRODUCTION, AFTERWORD, NOTES AND
ILLUSTRATIONS BY *NEW YORK TIMES* BEST-SELLING AUTHOR
BRADLEY TREVOR GREIVE

THOMAS DUNNE BOOKS
ST. MARTIN'S PRESS ✹ NEW YORK

THOMAS DUNNE BOOKS.
An imprint of St. Martin's Press.

For information, address St. Martin's Press,
175 Fifth Avenue, New York, N.Y. 10010.

www.thomasdunnebooks.com
www.stmartins.com

The Library of Congress Cataloging-in-Publication Data
is available upon request

ISBN 9781250098719 (hardcover)
ISBN 9781250098726 (e-book)

First printed in 2015. Reprinted in 2016 and 2017.
Published by arrangement with Taylor & Francis Group,
a trading division of Informa UK Limited.
First published in October 1932 by *Harper's Magazine*, New York.
First published in book form (*In Praise of Idleness and Other Essays*)
in 1935 by George Allen & Unwin Ltd, London.
In Praise of Idleness © 1996
The Bertrand Russell Peace Foundation Ltd, Nottingham.
Introduction, afterword, notes and illustrations © Bradley Trevor Greive.

Our books may be purchased in bulk for promotional, educational,
or business use. Please contact your local bookseller or the Macmillan
Corporate and Premium Sales Department at 1-800-221-7945, extension 5442,
or by e-mail at MacmillanSpecialMarkets@macmillan.com.

First published in Australia by Nero,
an imprint of Schwartz Publishing Pty Ltd

First U.S. Edition: June 2017
10 9 8 7 6 5 4 3 2 1

Cover design by Peter Long
Cover illustration courtesy of Hein Nouwens/Shutterstock
& Bradley Trevor Greive
Text design and typesetting by Peter Long & Tristan Main
Photo of Bertrand Russell: Corbis Images
Photo of Bradley Trevor Greive: Ken Scott

Printed in China by 1010 Printing International.

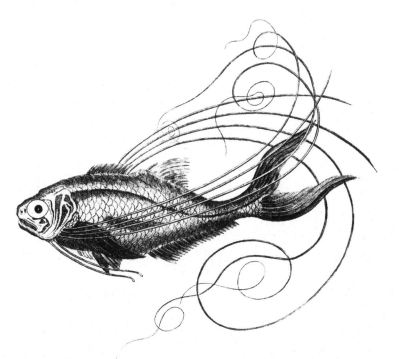

For Albert J. Zuckerman
God of books and brisket
King of cocktails
Last of the Literary Gentlemen
Manhattan Melampus who taught wild beasts
how to hold a pen
We cling to your moustache and are uplifted

"Men fear thought as they fear nothing else on earth – more than ruin, more even than death. Thought is subversive and revolutionary, destructive and terrible; thought is merciless to privilege, established institutions, and comfortable habits; thought is anarchic and lawless, indifferent to authority, careless of the well-tried wisdom of the ages. Thought looks into the pit of hell and is not afraid. It sees man, a feeble speck, surrounded by unfathomable depths of silence; yet it bears itself proudly, as unmoved as if it were lord of the universe. Thought is great and swift and free, the light of the world, and the chief glory of man." [1]

Bertrand Russell

ACKNOWLEDGMENTS

Acquiring permission to produce this special edition of *In Praise of Idleness* was a rather lengthy undertaking and I wish to publicly express my gratitude to the following people who went out of their way to aid my quest: Renu Barrett, Archivist at the Bertrand Russell Archives within the William Ready Division of Archives and Research Collections, McMaster University, Canada; Tony Simpson, of the Bertrand Russell Peace Foundation, England; and Adele Parker, of the Taylor & Francis Group, England.

When I first proposed this unusual collaboration a number of major publishers reached for their revolvers; not so with Nero and Black Inc. In my creative endeavours I received tremendous guidance and support from Jeanne Ryckmans and her talented team – I should like to make special mention of Samantha Forge, Siân Scott-Clash, Peter Long, Imogen Kandel, Caitlin Yates and Kelly Fagan.

That this book exists, and my modest publishing career remains extant, is entirely due to the grace and wisdom of my Literary Agent and Lord Protector – Al Zuckerman, of Writers House, New York, USA – without whom I would long ago have been exposed for the scabrous insect that I am.

Above all, heartfelt thanks are due to my brilliant and beautiful wife, Amy, who loves me in spite of my heroic flaws and also excused me from a great many wedding preparations so that I might finish my research.

To these extraordinary individuals, and almost every journalist, author and scholar who has written about Lord Russell during the past sesquicentury, I am in your debt.

B. T. G.

preface

CAME TO KNOW RUSSELL'S WORK LATER in life than most, though not so late as to not make a difference.

My first meaningful Russell encounter took place in New York a decade ago, when I was revelling in the bookish bacchanalia that is BookExpo America (BEA). My indefatigable American publicist was herding me from BEA to a promotional book-signing across town when my Brazilian publishers, Marcos and Tomas da Veiga

Pereira, commandeered our limousine as it pulled up outside the Javits Center and directed our driver into Midtown so they could buy tennis racquets.

Having effortlessly shrugged off their corporate responsibilities, Marcos and Tomas conversed happily with me (and my increasingly anxious publicist) about all manner of things, during the course of which (perhaps noting the wear and tear caused by my jet-schlepping lifestyle) they suggested I might enjoy reading *In Praise of Idleness*. Before leaping out of the car Marcos quickly wrote the essay title down on a sheet of notepaper in case I forgot – which I promptly did.

That same evening, just after midnight, having battled through a liver- and ego-bruising gauntlet of industry soirées, I ran into Marcos and Tomas again at a lavish BEA party. The handsome Brazilian brothers had stormed the dance floor with an unruly mob of independent booksellers from the

Atlantic Coast: two loose-hipped Latin gods gyrating within a writhing circle of bifocaled maenads. Other than a memory of being vaguely ashamed at how well I knew the words to a great many classic rock anthems, I'm not sure what happened next, but I regained consciousness at sunrise, courtesy of a brain-splitting telephone ring, when my publicist called my hotel room seeking proof of life. After a good deal of groaning, pained blinking and farting, I found I was lying on top of an unruffled bed, still dressed for quasi-serious literary business. However, my initial sense of relief was somewhat tempered by the subsequent discovery of a juicy half-eaten hamburger stuffed cruelly into my jacket pocket, the folded beef patty and deformed bun squished into a determined scowl. Compelled to anxiously probe all my pockets for additional trans-fat-dense fare, I fumbled across the crumpled piece of paper upon which Marcos had written the title of Russell's essay. Thank God.

When BEA concluded I flushed my system with aspirin and electrolytes and walked from Chelsea to Union Square, where I purchased *In Praise of Idleness and Other Essays* at the Barnes & Noble cathedral. I then strolled across the squirrel-infested park to the famous Coffee Shop, where I read the title essay once, twice, and then, just the ending for a third time. I was hooked.

Russell's message changed my life. Not immediately, perhaps – at least not visibly. But I started to look at my spare time differently, and then my time on earth in general. I tried to cut back on passive entertainment and move towards more active interests. Over the next ten years I travelled the world, founded a national poetry prize, participated in wildlife conservation programs on every continent, qualified to be a Russian cosmonaut in Moscow, competed in Polynesian strongman contests in Moorea and took up cooking, gardening and adventure-sports. Suffice to say, I ended up in hospital – following a dramatic high-speed desert racing accident – during which all my sponge-bath fantasies proved horribly misguided. Later I contracted chlamydia in my right eye when a koala urinated in my face. But I digress.

Between surgeries to repair my shattered right wrist, I learned how to write left-handed and even penned a humorous giftbook response to Russell's essay: *The Book For People Who Do Too Much*. Most importantly, I used my time in pyjama prison to read a good deal more of Russell's work and was beyond impressed by his original thinking, his exquisite writing and his ability to puncture bloated intellectual hubris and then spin complex contrary ideas into such succinct being that they could rest lightly on the point of the very same pin. I was similarly in awe of Russell's simple yet incredibly effective creative process; here was a proven approach to creative discipline at the highest level that anyone could employ to great effect. Russell's every neural impulse was an earthquake that rattled my tiny brain around inside my head like an oyster in a tumble dryer. His countless extraordinary achievements inspired me and, at the same time, made me feel unworthy to wear trousers.

Bertrand Russell was a monumental figure of 20th century philosophy – arguably the leading public intellectual of the "Era of Public Intellectuals" – whose influence, even today, extends far beyond the academic foundations of his fame. Immortalised in a poem by T. S. Eliot[2,3] and stories by D. H. Lawrence[4] and Aldous Huxley,[5,6,7] Russell mentored Ludwig Wittgenstein,[8,9,10] directly influenced Alan Turing[11] and The Beatles[12] and received fan mail from Albert Einstein.[13] In short: Russell was a genius who inspired other geniuses.[14]

Since first reading *In Praise of Idleness*, I have delivered many lectures on the nature of creativity, by which I mean creative thinking and also creative discipline. During these presentations I frequently refer to Bertrand Russell and to this essay in particular. Even in a large audience of talented creative professionals I would be happily stunned if more than fifty attendees knew of Lord Russell and his contributions to modern intellectual life. I've yet to find a room containing more than a dozen people who have read any of his celebrated essays, let alone *In Praise of Idleness*. Two or three hands in the air is the norm whenever I ask, and we can safely assume at least one proud arm is attached to a diamond-encrusted bullshitter.

Given how impactful Russell has been in my own life, I was determined to share his *sui generis* genius with as many people as possible and, having at last secured the blessing of the Bertrand Russell Peace Foundation, I present this modest volume to you.

I am neither a philosopher nor a mathematician and am known primarily for my humorous gift-books, so I do not pretend that I am worthy of this task. Nevertheless I feel honoured to have the opportunity to present Russell's work to a new audience. My only hope is that Russell's essay might afford you a similar epiphany to that which I experienced.

The highlighted quotes I have chosen – that you'll find scattered throughout – are among my personal favourites; however, their selection was also meant to indicate Russell's thinking on a variety of related subjects and to showcase the range of his notable writings.

The comic illustrations are only partly my original work, as they are essentially modified vintage wildlife etchings – mostly from the 17th, 18th and 19th centuries.[15] In any case, these lighthearted images are not vital to your reading experience, but are merely intended to offer visual relief while you are considering Russell's provocative words of wisdom.

Likewise, the notes I have provided are by no means essential to your enjoyment of Russell's essay, but I felt the work being presented demanded some form of reference for those who wish to venture further into Russell's oeuvre and examine his place in the historical record.[16]

When considering the asides and observations to include in the endnotes, I adopted Russell's advice on ideal mathematical notation: "A good [endnote] has a subtlety and suggestiveness which at times make it almost seem like a live teacher."[17] I hope that this additional information will help you connect with Russell's life, as well as with the great works of the many remarkable figures with whom he was associated, and also provide a sense of the dynamic times in which they lived.[18]

Finally, the brief afterword offers a biographical slice composed primarily to illustrate the development of Russell's creative process and to demonstrate the practical application of Active Idleness.

B. T. G.

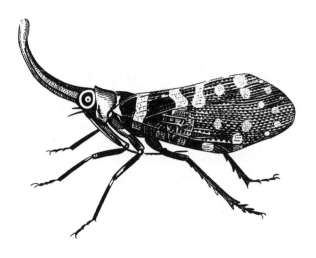

introduction

Great spirits have always encountered violent opposition from mediocre minds. The mediocre mind is incapable of understanding the man who refuses to bow blindly to conventional prejudices and chooses instead to express his opinions courageously and honestly.

– Albert Einstein

THE GREAT SPIRIT TO WHOM ALBERT Einstein is referring is Bertrand Russell. Einstein penned these inspiring and damning words in a letter to his dear friend, Morris Raphael Cohen,[19] venerable namesake of the Cohen Library at the City College of New York (CCNY), while championing the appointment of Russell to a teaching position at CCNY, in response to virulent opposition by a confederacy of offended Catholics and strident Episcopalians who feared Russell's controversial ideas would corrupt the young.[20]

That Russell was considered too radical for one of America's most creative and innovative university campuses says a great deal about how far ahead of his time he was. The greater point being twofold: Russell was much admired by the brightest minds of his day, and he remained resolutely unrepentant in advocating contrarian views.

Undersized, weathered and frequently dishevelled, at first glance Russell may not have struck you as the epitome of intellectual gravitas – BBC demigod Alistair Cooke once said that "From even a short distance [Russell] could fairly have been mistaken for a beggar".[21] Russell's almost perfect likeness to the Mad Hatter[22] was noted by his students[23] and, even in the most flattering photographs, the great philosopher often resembles a bewigged ferret squinting into a hot wind.

Russell's reputation as a liberal maverick was further compromised by his stiff manner, conservative dress code and odd voice, which was high, pinched and lightly dusted with gravel – an exasperated chain-smoking Mother Superior showing enormous restraint. There was almost nothing about Russell's person that might have been considered chic, cool, hot, hip or happening.

Of course anyone with even a passing interest in philosophy can appreciate that appearances are almost always deceptive – this scruffy little aristocrat was ferociously avant-garde in his day and his extraordinary legacy, including reams of revolutionary ideas, continues to dazzle our most brilliant minds and enrich countless lives.

Russell possessed a formidable intellect that he kept well employed throughout a long and charged passage of human history. In a lifetime that spanned the Māori Wars and the Moon landings, Russell saw, experienced, considered and contributed a very great deal.

He was a gannet-like guzzler of scientific, philosophical, political and cultural information, and was known to seek cerebral relief by tossing down mystery novels like breath mints; devouring two or more books in a sitting, in just fifteen minutes apiece.[24]

His angular cranium might best be imagined as the intellectual equivalent of Doctor Who's TARDIS, as it had a seemingly infinite capacity for complex ideas. A true polymath, Russell's intellectual powers were humbling, as was his heroic output, making enduring contributions to numerous academic fields.

That a mathematician cum philosopher should be awarded the Nobel Prize in Literature in 1950 sits very neatly, at least in terms of improbability, between the New Zealand physicist Ernest Rutherford receiving the Chemistry Nobel in 1908 and Sylvester Stallone's Academy Award nomination for Best Actor in 1977.[25]

The staggering scope of Russell's genius is difficult to measure, as he remains one of a kind.[26] We can speculate about his stature in comparison to the Ancients who first forged the remarkable tools from which we have assembled our collective intelligence, but certainly in the modern record there is no other mortal known to possess Russell's gifts for linguistic and mathematical mastery, let alone his deft manipulation of logic, which would have won him an ovation from every eminent figure in the *School of Athens*.[27]

Surprisingly, for someone who wrote over seventy books, penned thousands of papers and articles and delivered countless lectures and interviews, Russell was, in person, a man of few words, none of them wasted. Of course when obliged to speak up he invariably did so, never leaving any doubt as to where he stood in relation to the great questions of his day.

In addition to producing much of the framework for how we think about what we think about,[28] Russell also had an unerring sense of social justice that consistently placed him on the right side of history: he vocally championed women's rights and argued for same-sex equality when such views were deeply unpopular. He also condemned imperialism, racism, classism and slavery and was staunchly pro-democracy, despite his aristocratic background.

Though a lifelong pacifist, Russell's world-view was larger than most and, as he was absolutely not an absolutist, his positions were more nuanced. He was more than happy to lose his professorship at Cambridge and go to prison for his opposition to the First World War, which he felt was a tragic venture born of nationalist folly goaded by foam-mouthed militarist fools. However, while still opposed to violence, he argued there was every reason to obliterate the designs of Adolf Hitler, and publically condemned Lenin and Stalin as well. One of the very earliest critics of the Vietnam War, Russell ensured those nations and individuals responsible for atrocities committed in this Cold War proxy-conflict were called to account, resulting in the International War Crimes Tribunal which he organised with Jean-Paul Sartre in 1967.[29] From the detonation of the first atomic bomb till his final breath twenty-five years later, Russell remained committed to nuclear disarmament. His international activism resulted in his joining with Albert Einstein to produce *The Russell-Einstein Manifesto* in 1955; this powerful document, in turn, led to the creation of the famous Pugwash Conferences on Science and World Affairs, which began in 1957,[30] and also drove him to establish the Bertrand Russell Peace Foundation in 1963.

This is not to say that everything Russell wrote, said or did was right or without flaw – he received plenty of criticism from friends, family, journalists and less distinguished peers – not all of which was unjustified – along with a most impressive pile of poorly punctuated hate mail.[31]

Astonishingly and queasily enough, Russell was a certified lady-killer; a tweedy satyr, if you will. To be clear, Russell regarded women with great respect,[32] and his unwavering belief that women were entitled to absolute equality with men[33] was ahead of its time.[34] Nevertheless, his intimate relationships with women were frequently brief and fraught – Russell was not so much a hopeless romantic as a wrecking ball of love; leaving three wives, numerous affairs, and a great many angry and wounded lovers in his wake.[35]

A musky advocate for open marriage, Russell's sensuous appetite seemed almost insatiable, such that one might even nominate him as the vaguely pathetic Edwardian Oxbridge answer to Italy's Casanova, or even Hollywood's Warren Beatty, the Great Inseminator himself. Though Russell never approached a miniscule fraction of the almost 13,000 lovers Beatty is alleged to have bedded,[36] he still remains the only man I know of to have openly lusted after a Quaker.[37] While Beatty retired his lothario tear-away trousers aged fifty-five, Russell kept at it until he was eighty, when he finally found true love, great happiness and genuine contentment with his fourth wife, the magnificent Edith Finch.[38]

Suffice to say, Russell was a man who lived by his own rules. He famously quipped that "common sense is the metaphysics of savages",[39] invariably held conventional thinking in contempt and was always ready to turn the world on its head in the pursuit of truth, regardless of the consequences to his reputation, all of which he endured with a wry smile and his beloved pipe.

This brings us to consider the historical setting in which Russell wrote *In Praise Of Idleness*. In very broad terms the early 1930s could be described as an increasingly dark and difficult era strained by rival political ideologies, though occasionally brightened by technological innovation and artistic achievement. While the great drums were not yet booming to herald the Second World War, one could not help but notice an ominous buzz in the distance. And yet, almost ninety years before the rise of reality television and Justin Bieber, one looks back and imagines that it must, to some degree, have been a happier time.

Obviously a great deal happened in 1932,[40]

though, for our purposes, this historical window shall simply be viewed in the context of the Great Depression, which was still tumbling painfully towards its devastating nadir. One must be careful not to overstate the parallels to current conditions of economic uncertainty following the Global Financial Crisis of 2008, but it is at least fair to say that the situation then, as now, forced people to reconsider their views on traditional modes of employment, income and investment. Likewise, rapid advances in technology were transforming the social and professional milieu, as they are today. In the 1930s there existed, for some, many exciting opportunities; however, it was a time of great hardship and corrosive anxiety for most.

In Praise of Idleness is not one of Russell's most well-known or frequently quoted works – that honour goes to more provocative titles such as *Why Men Fight, The Problems of Philosophy, Why I Am Not a Christian* and *The Conquest of Happiness*. His two epic works on mathematical logic, *Principia Mathematica*[41] and *The Principles of Mathematics*, though famous for presenting Russell's greatest academic achievement and thus (along with *On Denoting*) embodying the cornerstone of his intellectual reputation, are so technical that they are seldom read outside of specialist corduroy-clad circles.[42] Likewise, it has become fashionable to mine Russell's three-volume autobiography for pithy quotes without reading the splendid work in its entirety. Nevertheless, even amid such illustrious tomes, *In Praise of Idleness* easily holds its own and affords an ideal opportunity to introduce (or reacquaint) the general reader to Bertrand Russell's inimitable, paradigm-shifting prose.

The essay can be divided into four basic sections: the illusion of wealth, the nature and history of work, the ethics of work and the importance of leisure.

After revealing a glimmer of his mischievous intelligence in his opening declaration that there is far too much work currently being done *and* that the belief that work is a noble endeavour is harmful, Russell immediately lurches into a feisty polemic against the traditional accumulation of wealth, implying that it invariably leads to cultural and moral poverty. Though this saucy gambit is by no means the most interesting part of Russell's essay, it is noteworthy and should be read and enjoyed, if only because doing so will upset investment bankers.

Having rolled up his sleeves, Russell offers the most brilliantly succinct definition of work ever conceived, and then delivers a swift historical account of labour and industry, the rise of technology and its implications, and the often painful division that exists and is perpetuated by those who provide and profit from (seemingly) essential labour. Russell argues that a redistribution of labour and its rewards is needed to break this divisive and unjust cycle in order for us to eradicate poverty and advance as a species.

Russell's forward thinking goes well beyond drastically reduced working hours (he proposes a four-hour day) and a lateral appreciation of the benefits yielded by improved production and distribution technologies. He valiantly breaks apart the arthritic knuckles that have held in place traditional workplace values first established by oppressive feudal lords that, to this day, ensure the rise of pungent plutocrats and a boom-bust cycle that shakes the very foundations of society.

At this point the careless reader[43] might dismiss Russell's unique brand of progressive socialism as vapid leftist idealism. However, Russell's views were not conceived in an Ivy League tower, but were born of real-world experience – Russell campaigned for free trade and open markets in 1903 and had no truck with undiluted communism, nationalism or socialism, having witnessed the malignant failure inherent in these idealistic political and socioeconomic systems (as a result of even the most minor corruption) during his many international travels; including extended visits to Soviet Russia and the Republic of China in 1920 and 1921.[44]

If one pays attention to the suggestions Russell offers in this passage, and also examines the manner in which he disposed of his inherited wealth and actively sought out, earned and spent his own income,[45] it's evident that Russell practised what he preached. Far from serving watered-down champagne socialism, it's clear that Russell was a charismatic champion of compassionate capitalism.

After comparing the attitudes behind the notion of *work as duty* as held in the USA and Russia (during Russell's day), it's evident to Russell that both points of view are ultimately detrimental.

Regardless of whether the driving ideology is socialist or capitalist, the end result is a modern slave
state where people spend their lives in endless toil
and passive entertainment, with little else besides.
Even an impassioned advocate for capitalism with
an inordinate fondness for excessive wealth must
concede that while free markets are important, personal freedom is everything.

Russell goes on to examine the ethics of
work and, while he acknowledges the essential benefits afforded by production, he ultimately asserts
that work as it is presently undertaken is harmful
for two basic, interrelated reasons: it denies us
leisure, and it diminishes our capacity for interesting thought.

Russell believes that excessive work (and our
obsession with same) degrades a person's mind –
assertions that neuroscientists have recently proven
to be accurate. For example multi-tasking, often a

point of pride for modern professionals, has been shown to lower our mental efficiency and result in impaired cognitive function that is worse than from smoking marijuana.[46] Likewise the constant deluge of digital information to which we are exposed can result in a debilitating form of neural addiction that gradually narrows our scope of meaningful achievement while creating the illusion that we are actually accomplishing more with our time.

As Russell foretold, the modern mind is constantly revving but rarely engaged in gear. Our jobs keep us busier and the technology is getting smarter while our brains are shrivelling and our imagination is fading. If we cannot find the time to think deeply – to plunge below the ripples of reactive thinking that flit across the surface of our conscious mind and create some genuine cerebral turbulence, from which we might generate original ideas and conceive the manner in which they can be brought to fruition, then our dreams will be lost in the incandescent spume of the digital age.[47]

And now the most significant and exciting part of Russell's essay – the vital importance of leisure and idleness. This should not be mistaken for passive idleness, such as when a dispirited corporate drone collapses in front of Netflix, gropes for greasy popcorn at the movies, fills an uncrowded quarter hour with a Twitter flame war, unloads his worries onto a barman, sizzles in a poolside puddle of sunscreen, or vanquishes a video game nemesis with his heroic opposable thumbs. Oh no.

Ideal leisure, according to Russell, is the product of civilisation and education. When used properly – by which he means actively – such leisure is the source of almost everything that makes life interesting and enjoyable. It is the wellspring from which the arts and sciences are drawn, the fount of almost all earth-shattering original ideas. Idleness gives us the opportunity to explore, taste and try new things. Such unfettered curiosity creates new interests, these become passions, and these passions set fire to the hearts and minds of those around us.

Idleness, as Russell states, makes people happy. It is essential to the capacity for light-heartedness and playfulness, which creates the ideal environment within which to discover hidden talents and learn new skills. Engaging in play offers easy access to one of the most creative states a person can attain, which is why having time to think about things for no reason other than that it delights and stimulates us is often the key to breakthrough ideas, and thus the path to genius and joy. And of course, as Russell points out, happy people are generally kinder people, and showing kindness also makes other people happier and, in turn, kinder. In essence, this positive cycle is the very definition of the virtuous circle.

Everything you admire, and everything anyone has ever created that inspires you is the result of their being able to step away from their pressing obligations and think really big – or really small, as the case may be. After reading Russell you can sense him demanding greater depth from our age of abundant creativity. He asks us to reject the recursive regurgitation of ideas that spawned a million Hollywood sequels, and instead stop, pause, relax, unclench our cerebrum, think differently, think deeply, and then take action.

Consider the great and wondrous things already realised before you and I existed and then imagine what might yet be accomplished if only we allow ourselves the mental space to conceive it. Conversely, if business and busyness prevent us from ever aspiring to such luminous endeavours, why, we may as well just shit ourselves lifeless and be done with it.

This is an inspiring and sobering wake-up call to make the most of our lives by doing a lot less: almost nothing in fact. Russell's argument is a call to action for every citizen of our age of ideas and, if applied, heralds the next wave of enlightened entrepreneurs.

Entertaining and thought-provoking, *In Praise of Idleness* is a must read for anyone brave enough to step away from the pedestrian grind and stare into the future void to behold a blank canvas upon which he or she can make their unique mark and, in doing so, delight the whole world for all time.

As Bertrand Russell wrote, "There are two motives for reading a book: One, that you enjoy it; the other, that you can boast about it."[48] In this slim volume, I believe, both motives are rewarded.

B. T. G.

In Praise of Idleness

by Bertrand Russell

L IKE MOST OF MY GENERATION, I WAS brought up on the saying: "Satan finds some mischief still for idle hands to do." Being a highly virtuous child, I believed all that I was told, and acquired a conscience which has kept me working hard down to the present moment. But although my conscience has controlled my actions, my opinions have undergone a revolution. I think that there is far too much work done in the world, that immense harm is caused by the belief that work is virtuous, and that what needs to be preached in modern industrial countries is quite different from what always has been preached. Everyone knows the story of the traveller in Naples who saw twelve beggars lying in the sun (it was before the days of Mussolini), and offered a lira to the laziest of them. Eleven of them jumped up to claim it, so he gave it to the twelfth.[49] This traveller was on the right lines. But in countries which do not enjoy Mediterranean sunshine idleness is more difficult, and a great public propaganda will be required to inaugurate it. I hope that, after reading the following pages, the leaders of the YMCA[50] will start a campaign to induce good young men to do nothing. If so, I shall not have lived in vain.

Before advancing my own arguments for laziness, I must dispose of one which I cannot accept. Whenever a person who already has enough to live on proposes to engage in some everyday kind of job, such as school-teaching or typing, he or she is told that such conduct takes the bread out of other people's mouths, and is therefore wicked. If this argument were valid, it would only be necessary for us all to be idle in order that we should all have our mouths full of bread. What people who say such things forget is that what a man earns he usually spends, and in spending he gives employment. As long as a man spends his income, he puts just as much bread into people's mouths in spending as he takes out of other people's mouths in earning. The real villain, from this point of view, is the man who saves. If he merely puts his savings in a stocking, like the proverbial French peasant, it is obvious that they do not give employment. If he invests his savings, the matter is less obvious, and different cases arise.

One of the commonest things to do with savings is to lend them to some Government. In view of the fact that the bulk of the public expenditure of most civilised Governments consists in payment for past wars or preparation for future wars, the man who lends his money to a Government is in the same position as the bad men in Shakespeare who hire murderers.[51] The net result of the man's economical habits is to increase the armed forces of the State to which he lends his savings. Obviously it would be better if he spent the money, even if he spent it on drink or gambling.

But, I shall be told, the case is quite different when savings are invested in industrial enterprises. When such enterprises succeed, and produce something useful, this may be conceded. In these days, however, no one will deny that most enterprises fail. That means that a large amount of human labour, which might have been devoted to producing something that could be enjoyed, was expended on producing machines which, when produced, lay idle

✳

"We all have a tendency to think that the world must conform to our prejudices. The opposite view involves some effort of thought, and most people would die sooner than think – in fact they do so."

The ABC of Relativity [1925]

✳

and did no good to anyone. The man who invests his savings in a concern that goes bankrupt is therefore injuring others as well as himself. If he spent his money, say, in giving parties for his friends, they (we may hope) would get pleasure, and so would all those upon whom he spent money, such as the butcher, the baker, and the bootlegger. But if he spends it (let us say) upon laying down rails for surface cars in some place where surface cars turn out to be not wanted, he has diverted a mass of labour into channels where it gives pleasure to no one.[52] Nevertheless, when he becomes poor through the failure of his investment he will be regarded as a victim of undeserved misfortune, whereas the gay spendthrift, who has spent his money philanthropically, will be despised as a fool and a frivolous person.

All this is only preliminary. I want to say, in all seriousness, that a great deal of harm is being done in the modern world by belief in the virtuousness of work, and that the road to happiness and prosperity lies in an organised diminution of work.

First of all: what is work? Work is of two kinds: first, altering the position of matter at or near the earth's surface relatively to other such matter; second, telling other people to do so. The first kind is unpleasant and ill paid; the second is pleasant and highly paid. The second kind is capable of indefinite extension: there are not only those who give orders, but those who give advice as to what orders should be given. Usually two opposite kinds of advice are given simultaneously by two organised bodies of men; this is called politics. The skill required for this kind of work is not knowledge of the subjects as to which advice is given, but knowledge of the art of persuasive speaking and writing, i.e. of advertising.

Throughout Europe, though not in America, there is a third class of men, more respected than either of the classes of workers. There are men who,

*

"The good life, as I conceive it, is a happy life. I do not mean that if you are good you will be happy; I mean that if you are happy you will be good."

New Hopes for a Changing World [1951]

*

through ownership of land, are able to make others pay for the privilege of being allowed to exist and to work. These landowners are idle, and I might therefore be expected to praise them. Unfortunately, their idleness is only rendered possible by the industry of others; indeed their desire for comfortable idleness is historically the source of the whole gospel of work. The last thing they have ever wished is that others should follow their example.

From the beginning of civilisation until the Industrial Revolution, a man could, as a rule, produce by hard work little more than was required for the subsistence of himself and his family, although his wife worked at least as hard as he did, and his children added their labour as soon as they were old enough to do so. The small surplus above bare necessaries was not left to those who produced it, but was appropriated by warriors and priests. In times of famine there was no surplus; the warriors and priests, however, still secured as much as at other times, with the result that many of the workers died of hunger. This system persisted in Russia until 1917,* and still persists in the East; in England, in spite of the Industrial Revolution, it remained in full force throughout the Napoleonic wars, and until a hundred years ago, when the new class of manufacturers acquired power. In America, the system came to an end with the Revolution, except in the South, where it persisted until the Civil War. A system which lasted so long and ended so recently has naturally left a profound impress upon men's thoughts and opinions. Much that we take for granted about the desirability of work is derived from this system, and, being pre-industrial, is not adapted to the modern world. Modern technique has made it possible for leisure, within limits, to be not the prerogative

---

* Since then, members of the Communist Party have succeeded to this privilege of the warriors and priests.

of small privileged classes, but a right evenly distributed throughout the community. The morality of work is the morality of slaves, and the modern world has no need of slavery.

It is obvious that, in primitive communities, peasants, left to themselves, would not have parted with the slender surplus upon which the warriors and priests subsisted, but would have either produced less or consumed more. At first, sheer force compelled them to produce and part with the surplus. Gradually, however, it was found possible to induce many of them to accept an ethic according to which it was their duty to work hard, although part of their work went to support others in idleness. By this means the amount of compulsion required was lessened, and the expenses of government were diminished. To this day, 99 per cent of British wage-earners would be genuinely shocked if it were proposed that the King[53] should not have a larger income than a working man. The conception of duty, speaking historically, has been a means used by the holders of power to induce others to live for the interests of their masters rather than for their own. Of course the holders of power conceal this fact from themselves by managing to believe that their interests are identical with the larger interests of humanity. Sometimes this is true; Athenian slave-owners, for instance, employed part of their leisure in making a permanent contribution to civilisation which would have been impossible under a just economic system. Leisure is essential to civilisation, and in former times leisure for the few was only rendered possible by the labours of the many. But their labours were valuable, not because work is good, but because leisure is good. And with modern technique it would be possible to distribute leisure justly without injury to civilisation. Modern technique has made it possible to diminish enormously

"Fear is the main source of superstition, and one of the main sources of cruelty. To conquer fear is the beginning of wisdom."

Unpopular Essays [1950]

the amount of labour required to secure the necessaries of life for everyone. This was made obvious during the war.[54] At that time all the men in the armed forces, all the men and women engaged in the production of munitions, all the men and women engaged in spying, war propaganda, or Government offices connected with the war, were withdrawn from productive occupations. In spite of this, the general level of physical well-being among unskilled wage-earners on the side of the Allies was higher than before or since. The significance of this fact was concealed by finance: borrowing made it appear as if the future was nourishing the present. But that, of course, would have been impossible; a man cannot eat a loaf of bread that does not yet exist. The war showed conclusively that, by the scientific organisation of production, it is possible to keep modern populations in fair comfort on a small part of the working capacity of the modern world. If, at the end of the war, the scientific organisation, which had been created in order to liberate men for fighting and munition work, had been preserved, and the hours of work had been cut down to four, all would have been well. Instead of that the old chaos was restored, those whose work was demanded were made to work long hours, and the rest were left to starve as unemployed. Why? Because work is a duty, and a man should not receive wages in proportion to what he has produced, but in proportion to his virtue as exemplified by his industry.

This is the morality of the Slave State, applied in circumstances totally unlike those in which it arose. No wonder the result has been disastrous. Let us take an illustration. Suppose that, at a given moment, a certain number of people are engaged in the manu-facture of pins. They make as many pins as the world needs, working (say) eight hours a day. Someone makes an invention by which the same number of

"When a man tells you that he knows the exact truth about anything, you are safe in inferring that he is an inexact man."

The Scientific Outlook [1931]

men can make twice as many pins as before. But the world does not need twice as many pins: pins are already so cheap that hardly any more will be bought at a lower price. In a sensible world, everybody concerned in the manufacture of pins would take to working four hours instead of eight, and everything else would go on as before. But in the actual world this would be thought demoralising. The men still work eight hours, there are too many pins, some employers go bankrupt, and half the men previously concerned in making pins are thrown out of work. There is, in the end, just as much leisure as on the other plan, but half the men are totally idle while half are still overworked. In this way, it is insured that the unavoidable leisure shall cause misery all round instead of being a universal source of happiness. Can anything more insane be imagined?[5]

The idea that the poor should have leisure has always been shocking to the rich. In England, in the early nineteenth century, fifteen hours was the ordinary day's work for a man; children some-times did as much, and very commonly did twelve hours a day. When meddle-some busybodies suggested that perhaps these hours were rather long, they were told that work kept adults from drink and children from mischief. When I was a child, shortly after urban working men had acquired the vote, certain public holidays were established by law, to the great indignation of the upper classes. I remember hearing an old Duchess say: "What do the poor want with holidays? They ought to work." People nowadays are less frank, but the sentiment persists, and is the source of much of our economic confusion.

Let us, for a moment, consider the ethics of work frankly, without superstition. Every human being, of necessity, consumes, in the course of his life, a certain amount of the produce of human labour. Assuming, as we may, that labour is on the whole disagreeable, it is unjust that a man should consume more than he produces. Of course he may provide services rather than commodities, like a medical man, for example; but he should provide something in return for his board and lodging. To this extent, the duty of work must be admitted, but to this extent only.

I shall not dwell upon the fact that, in all modern societies outside the USSR,[56] many people escape even this minimum amount of work, namely all those who inherit money and all those who marry money. I do not think the fact that these people are allowed to be idle is nearly so harmful as the fact that wage-earners are expected to overwork or starve.

If the ordinary wage-earner worked four hours a day, there would be enough for everybody, and no unemployment – assuming a certain very moderate amount of sensible organisation. This idea shocks the well-to-do, because they are convinced that the poor would not know how to use so much leisure. In America men often work long hours even when they are already well off; such men, naturally, are indignant at the idea of leisure for wage-earners, except as the grim punishment of unemployment; in fact, they dislike leisure even for their sons. Oddly enough, while they wish their sons to work so hard as to have no time to be civilised, they do not mind their wives and daughters having no work at all. The snobbish admiration of uselessness, which, in an aristocratic society, extends to both sexes, is, under a plutocracy, confined to women; this, however, does not make it any more in agreement with common sense.

The wise use of leisure, it must be conceded, is a product of civilisation and education. A man who has worked long hours all his life will be bored if he becomes suddenly idle. But without a considerable amount of leisure a man is cut off from many of the best things. There is no longer any reason why

*

"No one gossips about other people's secret virtues."

On Education [1926]

*

the bulk of the population should suffer this deprivation; only a foolish asceticism, usually vicarious, makes us continue to insist on work in excessive quantities now that the need no longer exists.

In the new creed which controls the government of Russia, while there is much that is very different from the traditional teaching of the West, there are some things that are quite unchanged. The attitude of the governing classes, and especially of those who conduct educational propaganda, on the subject of the dignity of labour, is almost exactly that which the governing classes of the world have always preached to what were called the "honest poor". Industry, sobriety, willingness to work long hours for distant advantages, even submissiveness to authority, all these reappear; moreover authority still represents the will of the Ruler of the Universe, Who, however, is now called by a new name, Dialectical Materialism.

The victory of the proletariat in Russia has some points in common with the victory of the feminists in some other countries. For ages, men had conceded the superior saintliness of women, and had consoled women for their inferiority by maintaining that saintliness is more desirable than power. At last the feminists decided that they would have both, since the pioneers among them believed all that the men had told them about the desirability of virtue, but not what they had told them about the worthlessness of political power. A similar thing has happened in Russia as regards manual work. For ages, the rich and their sycophants have written in praise of "honest toil", have praised the simple life, have professed a religion which teaches that the poor are much more likely to go to heaven than the rich, and in general have tried to make manual workers believe that there is some special nobility about altering the position of matter in space, just as men tried to make women believe that

"As soon as we abandon our own reason, and are content to rely upon authority, there is no end to our troubles."

Unpopular Essays [1950]

they derived some special nobility from their sexual enslavement. In Russia, all this teaching about the excellence of manual work has been taken seriously, with the result that the manual worker is more honoured than anyone else. What are, in essence, revivalist appeals are made, but not for the old purposes: they are made to secure shock workers for special tasks. Manual work is the ideal which is held before the young, and is the basis of all ethical teaching.

For the present, possibly, this is all to the good. A large country, full of natural resources, awaits development, and has to be developed with very little use of credit. In these circumstances, hard work is necessary, and is likely to bring a great reward. But what will happen when the point has been reached where everybody could be comfortable without working long hours?

In the West, we have various ways of dealing with this problem. We have no attempt at economic justice, so that a large proportion of the total produce goes to a small minority of the population, many of whom do no work at all. Owing to the absence of any central control over production, we produce hosts of things that are not wanted. We keep a large percentage of the working population idle, because we can dispense with their labour by making the others overwork. When all these methods prove inadequate, we have a war: we cause a number of people to manufacture high explosives, and a number of others to explode them, as if we were children who had just discovered fireworks. By a combination of all these devices we manage, though with difficulty, to keep alive the notion that a great deal of severe manual work must be the lot of the average man.

In Russia, owing to more economic justice and central control over production, the problem will have to be differently solved. The rational solution would be, as soon as the necessaries and elementary comforts can be provided for all, to reduce the hours of labour gradually, allowing a popular vote to decide, at each stage, whether more leisure or more goods were to be preferred. But, having taught the supreme virtue of hard work, it is difficult to see how the authorities can aim at a paradise in which there will be much leisure and little work. It seems more likely that they will find continually fresh schemes, by which present leisure is to be sacrificed to future productivity. I read recently of an ingenious plan put forward by Russian engineers, for making the White Sea and the northern coasts of Siberia warm, by putting a dam across the Kara Sea. An admirable project, but liable to postpone proletarian comfort for a generation, while the nobility of toil is being displayed amid the ice-fields and snowstorms of the Arctic Ocean. This sort of thing, if it happens, will be the result of regarding the virtue of hard work

"Men tend to have the beliefs that suit their passions. Cruel men believe in a cruel God, and use their belief to excuse their cruelty. Only kindly men believe in a kindly God, and they would be kindly in any case."

London Calling [1947]

as an end in itself, rather than as a means to a state of affairs in which it is no longer needed.

The fact is that moving matter about, while a certain amount of it is necessary to our existence, is emphatically not one of the ends of human life. If it were, we should have to consider every navvy superior to Shakespeare. We have been misled in this matter by two causes. One is the necessity of keeping the poor contented, which has led the rich, for thousands of years, to preach the dignity of labour, while taking care themselves to remain undignified in this respect. The other is the new pleasure in mechanism, which makes us delight in the astonishingly clever changes that we can produce on the earth's surface. Neither of these motives makes any great appeal to the actual worker. If you ask him what he thinks the best part of his life, he is not likely to say: "I enjoy manual work because it makes me feel that I am fulfilling man's noblest task, and because I like to think how much man can transform his planet. It is true that my body demands periods of rest, which I have to fill in as best I may, but I am never so happy as when the morning comes and I can return to the toil from which my contentment springs." I have never heard working men say this sort of thing. They consider work, as it should be considered, a necessary means to a livelihood, and it is from their leisure hours that they derive whatever happiness they may enjoy.

It will be said that, while a little leisure is pleasant, men would not know how to fill their days if they had only four hours of work out of the twenty-four. In so far as this is true in the modern world, it is a condemnation of our civilisation; it would not have been true at any earlier period. There was formerly a capacity for light-heartedness and play which has been to some extent inhibited by the cult of efficiency. The modern man thinks that everything ought to be done for the sake of something else, and never for its own sake. Serious-minded persons, for example, are continually condemning the habit of going to the cinema, and telling us that it leads the young into crime. But all the work that goes to producing a cinema is respectable, because it is work, and because it brings a money profit. The notion that the desirable activities are those that bring a profit has made everything topsy-turvy. The butcher who provides you with meat and the baker who provides you with bread are praiseworthy, because they are making money; but when you enjoy the food they have provided, you are merely frivolous, unless you eat only to get strength for your work. Broadly speaking, it is held that getting money is good and spending money is bad. Seeing that they are two sides of one transaction, this is absurd; one might as well maintain that keys are good, but key-holes are bad. Whatever merit there may be in the production of goods must be entirely derivative from the advantage to be obtained by consuming them. The individual, in our society, works for profit; but the social purpose of his work lies in the consumption of what he produces. It is this divorce between the individual and the social purpose of production that makes it so difficult for men to think clearly in a world in which profit-making is the incentive to industry. We think too much of production, and too little of consumption. One result is that we attach too little importance to enjoyment and simple happiness, and that we do not judge production by the pleasure that it gives to the consumer.

When I suggest that working hours should be reduced to four, I am not meaning to imply that all the remaining time should necessarily be spent in pure frivolity. I mean that four hours' work a day should entitle a man to the necessities and elementary comforts of life, and that the rest of his time

✳

"Cast-iron rules are above all things to be avoided."

On Education [1926]

✳

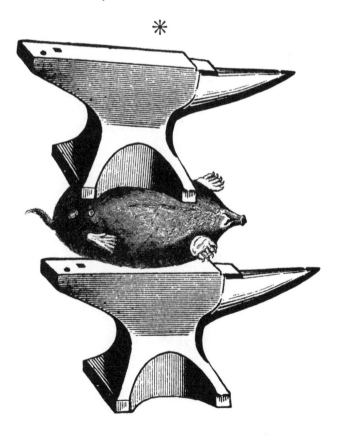

should be his to use as he might see fit. It is an essential part of any such social system that education should be carried further than it usually is at present, and should aim, in part, at providing tastes which would enable a man to use leisure intelligently. I am not thinking mainly of the sort of things that would be considered "highbrow". Peasant dances have died out except in remote rural areas, but the impulses which caused them to be cultivated must still exist in human nature. The pleasures of urban populations have become mainly passive: seeing cinemas, watching football matches, listening to the radio, and so on. This results from the fact that their active energies are fully taken up with work; if they had more leisure, they would again enjoy pleasures in which they took an active part.

In the past, there was a small leisure class and a larger working class. The leisure class enjoyed advantages for which there was no basis in social justice; this necessarily made it oppressive, limited its sympathies, and caused it to invent theories by which to justify its privileges. These facts greatly diminished its excellence, but in spite of this draw-back it contributed nearly the whole of what we call civilisation. It cultivated the arts and discov-ered the sciences; it wrote the books, invented the philosophies, and refined social relations. Even the liberation of the oppressed has usually been inaugurated from above. Without the leisure class, mankind would never have emerged from barbarism.

The method of a hereditary leisure class without duties was, however, extraordinarily waste-ful. None of the members of the class had been taught to be industrious, and the class as a whole was not exceptionally intelligent. The class might produce one Darwin, but against him had to be set tens of thousands of country gentlemen who never thought of anything more intelligent than

"The good life is one inspired by love and guided by knowledge."

An Outline of Philosophy [1927]

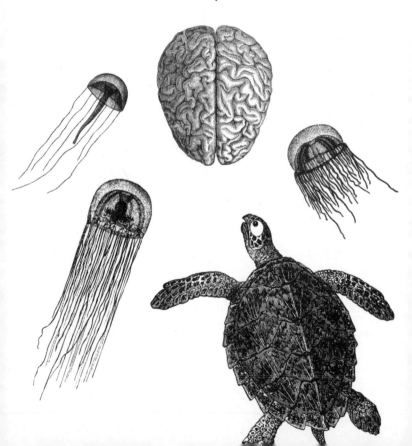

fox-hunting and punishing poachers. At present, the universities are supposed to provide, in a more systematic way, what the leisure class provided accidentally and as a by-product. This is a great improvement, but it has certain drawbacks. University life is so different from life in the world at large that men who live in an academic milieu tend to be unaware of the preoccupations and problems of ordinary men and women; moreover their ways of expressing themselves are usually such as to rob their opinions of the influence that they ought to have upon the general public. Another disadvantage is that in universities studies are organised, and the man who thinks of some original line of research is likely to be discouraged. Academic institutions, therefore, useful as they are, are not adequate guardians of the interests of civilisation in a world where everyone outside their walls is too busy for unutilitarian pursuits.

In a world where no one is compelled to work more than four hours a day, every person possessed of scientific curiosity will be able to indulge it, and every painter will be able to paint without starving, however excellent his pictures may be. Young writers will not be obliged to draw attention to themselves by sensational pot-boilers, with a view to acquiring the economic independence needed for monumental works, for which, when the time at last comes, they will have lost the taste and the capacity. Men who, in their professional work, have become interested in some phase of economics or government, will be able to develop their ideas without the academic detachment that makes the work of university economists often seem lacking in reality. Medical men will have time to learn about the progress of medicine, teachers will not be exasperatedly struggling to teach by routine methods things which they learnt in their youth, which may, in the interval, have been proved to be untrue.

Above all, there will be happiness and joy of life, instead of frayed nerves, weariness, and dyspepsia. The work exacted will be enough to make leisure delightful, but not enough to produce exhaustion. Since men will not be tired in their spare time, they will not demand only such amusements as are passive and vapid. At least one per cent will probably devote the time not spent in professional work to pursuits of some public importance, and, since they will not depend upon these pursuits for their livelihood, their originality will be unhampered, and there will be no need to conform to the standards set by elderly pundits. But it is not only in these exceptional cases that the advantages of leisure will appear. Ordinary men and women, having the opportunity of a happy life, will become more kindly and less persecuting and less inclined to view others with suspicion. The taste for war will die out, partly for this reason, and partly because it will involve long and severe work for all. Good nature is, of all moral qualities, the one that the world needs most, and good nature is the result of ease and security, not of a life of arduous struggle. Modern methods of production have given us the possibility of ease and security for all; we have chosen, instead, to have overwork for some and starvation for the others. Hitherto we have continued to be as energetic as we were before there were machines; in this we have been foolish, but there is no reason to go on being foolish forever.

Bertrand Russell

"Truth is a shining goddess, always veiled,
always distant, never wholly approachable,
but worthy of all the devotion of which
the human spirit is capable."

Fact and Fiction [1961]

✳

afterword

In Praise of Doubt

T HE BRITISH COUNTY OF MON-mouthshire must be considered the optimal birthplace for a freethinking analytic philosopher simply because no one can seem to agree where it actually is. Since Monmouthshire was brought into existence by Henry VIII this picturesque county was very definitely located in Wales, or in England, or in some unspecified third place that theoretically existed between or within both nations.[57] The one thing we know for certain about

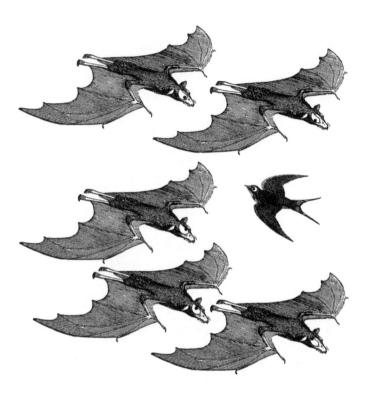

"Conventional people are roused to fury by departures from convention, largely because they regard such departures as a criticism of themselves."

The Conquest of Happiness [1930]

✳

Monmouthshire is that Bertrand Arthur William Russell drew his first breath there on Saturday the 18th of May, 1872.

"Bertie", as he was known to family and friends, was the youngest of three children. His brother, Frank, was almost seven years older and went on to be known, somewhat unfairly, as "The Wicked Earl", largely due to administrative confusion over his divorce status, which resulted in his arrest and subsequent conviction as a bigamist by a clique of Edwardian prudes.[58] His sister, Rachel, was four years older and tragically did not live long enough to be party to any scandal.

Russell's parents, the Viscount and Viscountess Amberley, could be regarded as the Victorian answer to Zelda and F. Scott Fitzgerald. This is not to say that Bertie's mother was a schizophrenic gin-monkey, nor his father an alcoholic puddle of fop-lit depression, but rather that "Lady Kate" and "Lord

John" were every bit as brilliant and self-destructive as Zelda and Scott. Both couples were injuriously progressive and died so young that neither lived up to their considerable potential.

The Viscount and Viscountess were ardent suffragists and vocal champions of women's education and women's rights. Their views in favour of contraception and sexual freedom frequently caused their peers to gag on their cucumber sandwiches, and their personal actions were even more shocking: Russell's mother took pity on her children's sexually frustrated biology tutor, Douglas Alexander Spalding,[59] who, having contracted tuberculosis, was unable to woo or marry. Lady Kate, with the blessing of her husband, entered into a sexual relationship with Spalding so that he might not die a virgin. However noble the intent of such carnal collusion this *ménage à trois* (with a Darwinian chicken researcher no less!), along with their emphatically turning their backs on the church and consorting with Americans (Americans!!!) caused irreparable damage to Lord and Lady Amberley's reputation, which undermined their social position, hobbled their political aspirations and drew venomous rebuke from their elevated circle – and even from Queen Victoria herself.[60]

Nevertheless, to suggest that Bertie was swaddled in radical nappies would be misleading. Russell's parents and sister died when he was very young, as did his celebrated atheist godfather, John Stuart Mill, and the aforementioned Spalding, also an atheist, who had been named as Bertie's co-guardian. Of all these, Russell retained no meaningful personal memories.[61] He came to know them largely through books, as we do today.[62]

A third atheist, the gifted bookbinder and typographer, T.J. Cobden-Sanderson, was nominated by Lord Amberley to care for his sons,[63] who, like Spalding, appeared to have been pre-qualified for the position by virtue of his also being madly in love with Bertie's late mother. The situation was all rather tragic, steamy and complicated. Suffice to say Bertie's Victorian grandparents would have none of it; they marshalled the finest legal minds in England to contest their late son's will in the Court of Chancery, where it was shredded into confetti.

And so, aged only three and a freshly minted orphan, Bertie was bundled off to Pembroke Lodge – a Georgian mansion in London's Richmond Park, gifted for life to his venerable grandfather by an appreciative if po-faced monarch in 1847.[64]

Bertie's paternal grandparents were quite something. Lord John, the first Earl Russell, was a 19th-century liberal juggernaut who was twice Prime Minister and the lead architect of the Great Reform Act. He also gave representative govern-ment to Australia and once travelled to Elba to console Napoleon. However, Lord John's influence

"All imitation is dangerous."

How I Write [1954]

over his grandson was minimal, as he died ten days after Bertie's sixth birthday. In his autobiography Russell merely remembers Lord John, well advanced in years, either being rolled around the garden in a Bath chair or reading in his room[65] – a warm soul, perhaps, but no more charismatic than, say, an exceptionally learned baked potato.

This left little Bertie in the care of his grandmother, Countess Frances Russell; known as "Lady Fanny" to those brave enough to accept her embrace. She was a whispering Scottish Presbyterian with close-set eyes, who was far more formidable than she initially appeared. A Victorian Puritan with a radical heart, Lady Fanny was given the codename "Deadly Nightshade" by her husband's parliamentary colleagues as a result of her darkly subtle influence over Lord John.[66]

In later years Russell came to admire many of his grandmother's qualities, especially her ferociously independent spirit, but it was ironic that the woman who loved him most as a child was the woman least capable of love. Lady Fanny cherished her youngest grandson but, like a corseted gorgon, she could sweep the joy from the room with a glance and once told Bertie, as a teary six-year-old mourning the loss of his mother and father, that he was quite fortunate his wayward parents had died.

It was the terrifying Lady Fanny who hovered over Bertie; a pious, sotto-voiced spectre, constantly advocating prayer, study, chastity and good posture, and wholly forbidding sloth, blasphemy and the consumption of fresh fruit.[67]

This is not to say that young Bertie lacked for male role models: on his mother's side his uncles were, respectively, a Muslim, an Atheist and a Bishop. And on his father's side one uncle was a reclusive, near-blind, socially crippled meteorologist[68] and the other a former army lieutenant who had gone insane (and strangled a homeless man) after his fellow cavalry officers had arranged that he be attacked by a bear as a joke. All of which is to say that, at least in terms of how I understand the nature of the British aristocracy, Russell probably fared better than most.

With his parents and sister dead and his incorrigible elder brother sent away to boarding school, Bertie was left to endure a childhood that wasn't. It would be simplistic to say that from this crucible of grief emerged a lonely, quiet, solemn little boy who rapidly lost faith in Santa Claus and then God – because, while this is true, it glosses over an important phase in Russell's intellectual development.

As a young boy Russell read broadly and took his lessons seriously but, rather than remain indoors and be ruled by Lady Fanny's tiny iron fist, he frequently escaped and took sanctuary in the eleven acres of unkempt gardens that surrounded

*

"There is an artist imprisoned in each one of us. Let him loose to spread joy everywhere."

Untitled [*Bertrand Russell's last essay*] [1967]

*

Pembroke Lodge. Here he would go for long walks, lost in his own thoughts, able to freely consider the merits of his guardian's teachings, and let his mind wander from the lessons imparted by a parade of Germanic tutors and enter a state of Active Idleness.

Russell would later describe the solitary hours spent in the garden as the most important of his childhood.[69] As he meandered across meadows, climbed trees and hid among the hedgerows – collecting birds eggs, watching butterflies and identifying English flora and fauna – this remarkable little boy did not often let his mind go to waste on trivial pursuits,[70] but instead began to establish the deep thinking habits born of what he would later call "fruitful monotony", when apparent boredom transforms the seemingly idle brain into a powerful tool capable of generating bold new ideas, and is thus the very essence of *In Praise of Idleness*.

It was in the wilding gardens of Pembroke

Lodge, adrift in deep thought, that young Bertrand found the beginnings of his intellectual self that would be realised, many years later, as the world's Philosopher-Statesman in residence. The key point being that in addition to serious and purposeful study, Bertie needed to escape the overbearing influence of his guardian and tutors and the oppressive rigors of his domestic situation, so as to think for himself.

As Russell matured he took nothing for granted, questioning the nature and existence of God, the purpose and impact of religion and the logical foundations of geometry. The dashing figure Bertie chose as his masculine ideal was the great English Romantic poet, Percy Bysshe Shelley, a man whose rebellious verve was manifested in superb artistry, unrepentant social radicalism, a passion for science and reason, and a breathless commitment to the bedroom arts. All of which ensured that Shelley was reviled by Lady Fanny.

"Do not fear to be eccentric in opinion, for every opinion now accepted was once eccentric."

A Liberal Decalogue [1954]

Bertie was fifteen when he first stumbled upon Shelley's poetry and he was immediately and utterly "entranced". Through Shelley's poems Russell felt he had finally found a friend and mentor, a "kindred spirit, gifted as I never hoped to be with the power of finding words as beautiful as his thoughts". When not squeezing pimples the adolescent Russell spent virtually all of his spare time reading Shelley's works and learning the poems by heart – all without his grandmother's knowledge. He grew to love and admire this poet who seemed able to see and say things that the rest of the world could not. In his dreams the teenager tried to imagine what a personal audience with his idol would have been like, and would "wonder whether [he] should ever meet any live human being with whom [he] should feel so much in sympathy".[71]

It's not uncommon for children to embrace as idols figures their parents and teachers do not approve of, though it's hard to imagine a better choice of inspiration for someone destined to become one of the world's leading thinkers than Percy Bysshe Shelley. One wonders what might have become of Russell had he instead become enamoured with the volatile British explorer Sir Richard Francis Burton (at the peak of his fame when Russell was a young man) and been inspired to cut off the tip of his penis with a hunting knife and follow in the wild man's enormous boot prints. Luckily, he chose Shelley.

For such a passionate and inquisitive boy to be cloistered within Victorian petticoats must have been unbearable. Russell felt he could trust no one with his deeply personal and often iconoclastic thoughts, and began to keep a secret diary, cunningly labelled "Greek Exercises", and within which he wrote down his personal reflections in code, using English spelling composed of Ancient Greek letters. Among the perspicacious insights, he wrote in 1888, aged sixteen; "My whole religion is this: do every duty, and expect no reward for it, either here or hereafter."[72]

While giving his family only a modest indication of the genius he would soon become, young Russell quickly surpassed the intellectual reach of his grandmother and life at Pembroke Lodge became increasingly tense and awkward. One can easily imagine the deathly pauses following Bertie's dinner table heresies and perhaps even visualise Lady Fanny's furiously pursed puritan mouth resembling an especially retentive cat's anus being forced, against its will, to accept a penny.

Though he cherished private time to think, Bertie suffered greatly from loneliness in his teens and contemplated suicide on a number of occasions. Thankfully his tortured adolescent life was saved by what seemed to him a thrilling immersion into the world of mathematics, his ongoing love of nature,

Shelley's magnificent verse and a timely discovery of masturbation. Which, apart from his obsession with arithmetic, poetry and verdant shrubbery seems quite relatable, even today.

Lady Fanny, oblivious to Bertie's secret inner life, imagined a political future for her painfully polite grandson, not only that he might fill the hand-made Oxfords of his noble grandfather (and the raunchy Wildsmith loafers of his feckless father), but that young Bertie might continue a Russell family tradition that can be traced back to the Tudor period. For all her faults Lady Fanny did her best to groom the bookish youth for greatness and, in a way, she succeeded beyond her wildest dreams (and also beyond her worst nightmares).

But Russell didn't feel cut out for conventional public service – an opinion that was confirmed by a brief stint as an honorary attaché with the British Embassy in Paris in 1894, where, according

"A generation that cannot endure boredom will be a generation of little men, of men unduly divorced from the slow processes of nature, of men in whom every vital impulse slowly withers, as though they were cut flowers in a vase."

The Conquest of Happiness [1930]

to Russell's own account, he spent most of his time writing long dispatches in the hope of persuading the French Government "that a lobster is not a fish".

The most enduring piece of advice proffered by Lady Fanny, indeed one that stayed with Russell throughout his life, was a scriptural quote penned onto the fly-leaf of a King James Bible she gifted him as a child – it read, "Thou shall not follow a multitude to do evil".[73] These nine words empowered Russell to never feel amiss when standing apart from majority opinion, and can be felt in almost every aspect of his written work and public life.

When he arrived at Cambridge Russell suddenly burst into full bloom. Here, blessed with a splendid moustache and free from his grandmother's musty skirts, he could stretch his cerebral legs and run like a joyous colt in an endless field of wild ideas. In this safe, stimulating and encouraging environment he was able to deploy his original thinking to full effect, resulting in immediate academic success, achieving scholastic distinction in both mathematics and philosophy.

But it wasn't until after he graduated and was a Cambridge lecturer himself that he found the balanced approach that resulted in a creative discipline that suited him best, and helped him become one of the most prolific and important writers of all time.

It's now hard to imagine Russell ever encountering writer's block, especially considering he averaged some three thousand handwritten words per day throughout his life,[74] even while travelling, convalescing or in prison.[75] But nevertheless, there were occasions when, as a young man, Russell felt like he had reached a creative impasse. At such times inspiration would not yield, even to Russell's formidable intellect and resolute determination.

Initially, when trying to make a breakthrough in his work, Russell would hunker down at his desk

"Civilised life has grown altogether too tame."

Nobel Lecture: What Desires Are Politically Important? [1950]

and grind it out – doing almost nothing but studying, thinking and writing with increasing desperation. This came to a head at the end of 1913 when he was trying to prepare the series of Lowell Lectures he was to publish as a book and subsequently deliver to a packed house at MIT in Boston in the New Year, and he described his climacteric state as follows: "I concentrated with such intensity that I sometimes forgot to breathe and emerged panting as from a trance."[76]

Nevertheless, despite this immense commitment, the situation felt hopeless: Sisyphus at a typewriter.[77] Russell made no meaningful progress until he stepped away from his desk and gave his mind a chance to unravel the complex knots of information and artistic visions tangled up inside his head.

Perhaps recalling his days in the gardens of Pembroke Lodge, Russell realised a break was needed – he travelled to Rome for the Christmas holidays to unwind and recharge, and it worked. When he came back to Cambridge, despite now being under even greater pressure to deliver, he was able to dictate his entire book to an assistant right off the top of his head. Astonishing, but true.[78]

Russell later described this creative approach as follows: "Every one who has done any creative work has experienced, in a greater or less degree, the state of mind in which, after long labour, truth or beauty appears, or seems to appear in a sudden glory – it may be only about some small matter, or it may be about the universe ... I think most of the best creative work, in art, in science, in literature, and in philosophy, has been the result of such a moment ... For my part, I have found that when I wish to write a book on some subject, I must first soak myself in detail, until all the separate parts of the subject-matter are familiar; then, some day, if I am fortunate, I perceive the whole, with all its parts duly interrelated. After that, I only have to write down what I have seen. The nearest analogy is first walking all over a mountain in a mist, until every path and ridge and valley is separately familiar, and then, from a distance, seeing the mountain whole and clear in bright sunshine."[79] Russell goes on to add that after experiencing such creative insights, however miraculous, the work produced must be "tested soberly", which is to say editorial diligence must be applied before the work can be considered complete.

This then is a summary of the Russell Method of Creative Discipline:

- Exhaustive research and thought to the point of complete immersion in the subject.

- Attaining physical and objective distance from the project, during which further contemplation is undertaken in a state of Active Idleness.

"Even when the experts all agree, they may well be mistaken."

The Collected Papers of Bertrand Russell [1927–42]

- Seeing the work or solution as a whole, and reproducing same.

- Sober self-criticism and editing after the fact to ensure the creative and intellectual integrity of the project.

This combination of study, escape, contemplation, inspiration and critical evaluation makes perfect sense and served the prolific Russell well; to wit, without escape from the cerebral churn Russell could not find the freedom to think creatively, and without the intensely disciplined study he had nothing of substance to think about in the first place.

A number of famous authors since Russell have shared similar working methods, including Hemingway – who, when based in Cuba and Key West, would abandon his writing each afternoon to go fishing and allow his mind to drift clear of the novel in progress.

But there's more to this process than I've described – we are missing the essential ingredient that made Bertrand Russell, Bertrand Russell: doubt. He absolutely refused to accept commonly held opinions, however well established, without first considering them for himself.

As a thinker Russell was without fear – never mind rocking the boat, Russell was happy to sink the boat if what he was seeking lay on the ocean floor. There is no view he wouldn't contemplate, champion or oppose if doing so led him closer to a summit of art and reason. He was bold, creative and relentless. In short, Russell embraced life as an intellectual adventure.

The word "philosophy", derived from Ancient Greek and given to us by Pythagoras,[80] means "Love of Wisdom", and it was to this noble passion that Bertrand Russell dedicated his life. In order to move towards knowledge and understanding Russell first accepted that he knew and understood little, and could not trust prevailing views without rigorous proof. Ultimately what made Russell a more gifted thinker than most – and by *most* I mean virtually everybody who has ever lived – is that he was happy to be unsure or indeed proved wrong. As importantly, Russell never believed he alone had all the answers, or that meaningful answers could always in fact be found. Doubt and uncertainty were central elements to Russell's genius and thus are worthy of consideration for us all. There is great progress to be made in every aspect of life and work, especially in regards to creativity and innovation, if we can put into practice Russell's advice that, "In all affairs it's a healthy thing now and then to hang a question mark on the things you have long taken for granted."[81]

The scope of Russell's work is vast – enough to fill the résumés of three or more distinguished professors – but if there is a single thread that ties it all together, then it is the positive application of

"A truly robust morality can only be strengthened by the fullest knowledge of what really happens in the world."

On Education [1926]

doubt: Russell's unrelenting search for the kernels of truth that lie buried beneath layers of ignorance, human error, misunderstanding and mythology.

Though initially used to illustrate his views on the nature of seemingly irrefutable religious doctrine, Russell's famous "Celestial Teapot" analogy is an excellent example of the burden of proof he felt essential to ascertain truth; not just in relation to unfalsifiable religious beliefs, but also in regards to statements of "fact" in philosophy, mathematics and science which are often blindly accepted by the masses:

> *If I were to suggest that between the Earth and Mars there is a china teapot revolving about the sun in an elliptical orbit, nobody would be able to disprove my assertion provided I were careful to add that the teapot is too small to be revealed even by our most powerful telescopes. But if I were to go on to say that, since my assertion cannot be*

disproved, it is intolerable presumption on the part of human reason to doubt it, I should rightly be thought to be talking nonsense. If, however, the existence of such a teapot were affirmed in ancient books, taught as the sacred truth every Sunday, and instilled into the minds of children at school, hesitation to believe in its existence would become a mark of eccentricity and entitle the doubter to the attentions of the psychiatrist in an enlightened age or of the Inquisitor in an earlier time.[82]

In essence – you are never obliged to accept something as true just because you cannot immediately disprove it.

Throughout his career Russell applied systematic doubt – most probably inspired, at least in part, by René Descartes, the founder of modern philosophy – to countless mathematic, scientific, logical and philosophical problems, as well as ethical investigations into the human condition. In Russell's pursuit of knowledge there was nothing he wouldn't call into question, often with controversial results – so it's hardly surprising that thought leaders of Russell's day were uncomfortable to observe someone capable of disassembling the foundations of their existence.

Russell's greatness as a thinker, a writer and a champion for the oppressed was, in large part, derived from confidence born of doubt. Therefore to complete the Russell Method of Creative Discipline you need to add one more step at the very beginning:

• Question everything.

To elucidate Russell's position on the nature and importance of doubt – which is far more nuanced and inspiring than Descartes' – I invite you to dip into the first and final paragraphs from *The Problems of Philosophy* (1912).

✳

"What is wanted is not the will-to-believe, but the wish to find out, which is the exact opposite."

Free Thought and Official Propaganda [1922]

✳

Is there any knowledge in the world which is so certain that no reasonable man could doubt it? This question, which at first sight might not seem difficult, is really one of the most difficult that can be asked. When we have realised the obstacles in the way of a straightforward and confident answer, we shall be well launched on the study of philosophy, for philosophy is merely the attempt to answer such ultimate questions, not carelessly and dogmatically, as we do in ordinary life and even in the sciences, but critically, after exploring all that makes such questions puzzling, and after realising all the vagueness and confusion that underlie our ordinary ideas ... Philosophy is to be studied, not for the sake of any definite answers to its questions, since no definite answers can, as a rule, be known to be true, but rather for the sake of the questions themselves; because these questions enlarge our conception of what is possible, enrich our intellectual imagination and diminish the dogmatic assurance which closes the mind against speculation; but above all because, through the greatness of the universe which philosophy contemplates, the mind also is rendered great, and becomes capable of that union with the universe which constitutes its highest good.[83]

Bertrand Russell did many extraordinary things that were motivated by the highest good, but he was still just a man. He made mistakes, was humiliated and at times vilified, his major contribution to mathematics was proven to be flawed, he couldn't even manage to die until his third attempt,[84] and he maintained a splendid list of vices – intelligent women, tobacco, mystery novels and scotch whisky.

In his later years Russell was said to enjoy up to seven double-glasses of scotch a day: Red Hackle was his favourite poison – a whisky label as unpretentious as the philosopher himself.[85] That said, Russell

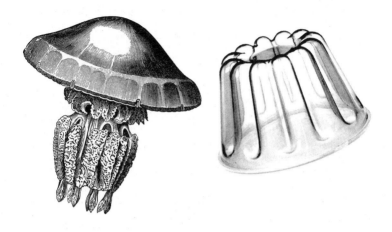

✳

"Most of the greatest evils that man has inflicted upon man have come through people feeling quite certain about something which, in fact, was false."

Unpopular Essays [1950]

✳

was not without moments of epic hubris. During the Cuban Missile Crisis in 1962, Russell dashed off impassioned cables to US President John F. Kennedy and Soviet supremo Nikita Khrushchev, strongly urging them to resolve the conflict with words not weapons – and later had the nerve to take some credit for the peaceful resolution of this tense stand-off, despite JFK rebuffing him in no uncertain terms.[86]

Nevertheless, while he seldom questioned his intellectual standing and influence, Russell approached his craft from a position of humility and appreciated the absurdity of life and the inherent difficulties found in the pursuit of truth, justice and meaning. As he once wrote, "That I, a funny little gesticulating animal on two legs, should stand beneath the stars and declaim in a passion about my rights – it seems so laughable, so out of all proportion."[87]

Nonetheless, this funny little gesticulating animal was a great champion for humankind:

pugnacious and eloquent, clear-eyed and compassionate, Russell possessed the mind of a scientist and the heart of a poet. We may never see his like again.

As I read Russell's books I half suspect that five hundred years from now cynical scholars in a less literate age will debate the authorship of Russell's titanic corpus just as we do the works of Shakespeare. It's not that Russell's voice changes – though his opinions do, steadily, whenever he reviewed his positions against new knowledge and found them wanting[88] – but rather it doesn't seem possible that any one person could have undertaken so many gruelling intellectual challenges for such an extended length of time, often against the overwhelming tides of popular and academic opinion.

What could have compelled Bertrand Russell to face doubt for so long, and to stand alone so often? To answer that question it is appropriate to close this modest, but I hope rewarding, little book

"The ontological argument and most of its refutations are found to depend on bad grammar."

Logical Atomism [1924]

with Russell's own words; written on the 25th of July, 1956, as the prologue to his autobiography, *What I Have Lived For*.[89]

Three passions, simple but overwhelmingly strong, have governed my life: the longing for love, the search for knowledge, and unbearable pity for the suffering of mankind. These passions, like great winds, have blown me hither and thither, in a wayward course, over a deep ocean of anguish, reaching to the very verge of despair.

I have sought love, first, because it brings ecstasy – ecstasy so great that I would often have sacrificed all the rest of life for a few hours of this joy. I have sought it, next, because it relieves loneliness – that terrible loneliness in which one shivering consciousness looks over the rim of the world into the cold unfathomable lifeless abyss. I have sought it, finally, because in the union of love I have seen, in a mystic miniature, the prefiguring vision of the heaven that saints and poets have imagined. This is what I sought, and though it might seem too good for human life, this is what – at last – I have found.

With equal passion I have sought knowledge. I have wished to understand the hearts of men. I have wished to know why the stars shine. And I have tried to apprehend the Pythagorean power by which number holds sway above the flux. A little of this, but not much, I have achieved.

Love and knowledge, so far as they were possible, led upward toward the heavens. But always pity brought me back to earth. Echoes of cries of pain reverberate in my heart. Children in famine, victims tortured by oppressors, helpless old people a hated burden to their sons, and the whole world of loneliness, poverty, and pain make a mockery of what human life should be. I long to alleviate the evil, but I cannot, and I too suffer.

"Anything you're good at contributes to happiness."

Bertrand Russell Speaks His Mind [1969]

✳

This has been my life. I have found it worth living, and would gladly live it again if the chance were offered me.[90]

Lord Russell died at 8pm, on Monday the 2nd of February, 1970, at *Plas Penrhyn*, in Penrhyndeudraeth, Wales – the unassuming country house where he had chosen to spend his final years, in large part because he could gaze across the green valley and see Tan-y-Ralt, Shelley's former home. In accordance with his final wishes, Russell's body was cremated without ceremony and his ashes scattered over the Snowdonia Mountains.

In his ninety-seven years Bertrand Russell did as much as any man has ever done to make our world a kinder and more intelligent planet.

B. T. G.

*

"The demand for certainty is one which is natural to man, but is nevertheless an intellectual vice ... To endure uncertainty is difficult, but so are most of the other virtues."

Unpopular Essays [1950]

*

[escalated]
further reading

Bertrand Russell: Philosophy in an Hour
by Paul Strathern
HarperPress (2012)

THE MOST AFFORDABLE BLUFFER'S GUIDE
on the market, this unbedizened sliver of biography
offers a tantalising glimpse into the life and work
of Russell that will enable you to smile and nod at
the periphery of an in-depth dinner conversation
between more learned friends without looking like
a complete idiot.

Logicomix: An Epic Search for Truth
by Apostolos Doxiadis, Christos H. Papadimitriou,
Alecos Papadatos and Annie Di Donna
Bloomsbury (2009)

EVEN AS A FORMER CARTOONIST DESPERATE to have my genius acknowledged, I find the term "graphic novel" unbearably pretentious – and don't even start me on meta-writings – nevertheless, I concede that this fun and rewarding book offers a fresh visual approach to some pretty weighty subject matter and is, on the whole, very enjoyable. It is definitely not reserved for semi-literate teenagers and slovenly thirty-somethings who still live with their parents, though certainly an ideal gift for same.

Bertrand Russell
by A. J. Ayer
University Of Chicago Press (1988)

A. J. AYER'S EXCELLENT BIOGRAPHY-IN-BRIEF benefits from and is flawed by the fact that Ayer was not only a close friend and great admirer of Russell's, but that his own academic triumphs descend directly from Russell's work. Indeed, one might say that Ayer sought the mantle of Russell's intellectual heir as desperately as Wittgenstein wished to shed it. With that caveat on record, and while acknowledging that this book is no longer readily available, I commend it to you as a wonderfully compact conspectus from one of modern philosophy's great characters.[91]

Russell: A Very Short Introduction
by A. C. Grayling
Oxford University Press (2002)

POUND FOR POUND THE BEST GENERAL introduction to Russell available today. This pocket volume delivers a crisp and succinct survey of every aspect of Russell's monumental life. Like Tyrion Lannister in *Game Of Thrones*, this fabulous runtling turns out to be far more impressive than it first appears.

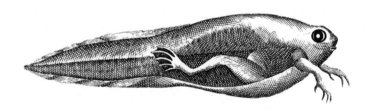

Autobiography
by Bertrand Russell
Routledge Classics (2009)

THERE SIMPLY IS NO BETTER WAY TO GET TO know Bertrand Russell than by reading his own three-volume account of his extraordinary life. Now available in a single edition, Russell's autobiography is honest, provocative, often hilarious and a joy to read. The sweep of Russell's journey, accomplishments, observations and influence is breathtaking (aided by the inclusion of correspondence with friends, family and countless notable persons). And, as the final instalment was completed only a year before his death, it has a profound sense of completion that few personal stories ever attain. One of the best autobiographies you will ever read.

Bertrand Russell: The Spirit
of Solitude 1872-1921 & Bertrand Russell:
The Ghost of Madness 1921-1970
by Ray Monk
Jonathan Cape (1996, 2000)

FOR A CONTRARY OPINION ON RUSSELL'S LIFE,
you cannot go past Ray Monk's double-barrelled
biography. It must be said that there are those, including myself, who feel Monk's portrait is excessively
focused on the less savoury aspects of Russell's personal life and, in addition, seems tainted by a curious
and petty hostility towards his subject that can only
partly be explained by the author's apparent devotion
to Wittgenstein. Nevertheless, Monk, unlike some
other leading Russell biographers (something he is
at undignified pains to point out), understands the
technical aspects of Russell's work, and this special-
ised knowledge adds an important dimension to a
comprehensive if overly critical biography.

Bertrand Russell's Best

&

The Basic Writings of Bertrand Russell
Routledge Classics (2009)

IF YOU'RE READY TO DIVE RIGHT INTO Russell's glittering oeuvre, then you are well advised to begin with these wonderful collections of shorter works, which include many of Russell's best essays, as selected by the great man himself. The two volumes overlap somewhat, so it basically comes down to appetite and wrist strength. The smaller book is essentially an *amuse-bouche* for your brain – it contains accessible works that will soon have you gasping, laughing and generally wishing you'd bought the larger volume. Speaking of which, don't be put off by the Brobdingnagian heft of this cerebral compendium – the essays within are composed with such intellectual verve and lightness of wit that you will find yourself wanting more.

A History of Western Philosophy
by Bertrand Russell
Simon & Schuster (2007)

NOW FOR THE MAIN COURSE: *A History of Western Philosophy* is a classic for good reason. Specifically cited by the Swedish Academy when presenting Russell with the Nobel Prize in Literature, it remains the most readable introduction to the principal schools of philosophy ever written and, in addition, Russell provides the historical and social context to help explain how and why the intelligent world came to be the way it is. At roughly nine hundred pages and the weight of a human head, this volume looks intimidating but in fact you'll be surprised how quickly you devour the whole thing and are ready for dessert.

The Conquest of Happiness
by Bertrand Russell
Liveright (2013)

SPEAKING OF DESSERT, THIS SLENDER volume is an invigorating ice-cream sundae with a cherry on top. An uplifting and thoughtful examination of what it means to be happy and how such a state can be obtained in the modern world. Russell's admission that he was not born happy, and indeed contemplated suicide many times, sets the stage for a truly unique examination of the subject as seen through the lens of his life journey. When you finally put down this wonderful book, you will be a new and better person ... which is great, though you should still seek a second opinion before you do anything drastic with your hair.

Portraits from Memory
and Other Essays
by Bertrand Russell
Spokesman Books (1995)

NOW YOU ARE JUST BEING GREEDY. This rare book is the cherry on top of another cherry, sprinkled with sugar and/or cocaine. In this volume, first published in the 1950s, Russell reveals a great deal more about his family history and his own relationships with and opinions of a number of celebrated historical figures, including George Santayana, D. H. Lawrence, John Stuart Mill and Joseph Conrad to name but a few. *Portraits from Memory* is not the easiest book to find but is certainly well worth the energy expended in obtaining it.

The Problems of Philosophy
by Bertrand Russell
Oxford Paperbacks (2001)

A FINAL BONUS SUGGESTION FOR INSATIABLE knowledge-monsters: *The Problems of Philosophy* is thought by many to be Russell's best work. Written in 1912 when Russell, well and truly established atop the international academic summit, was "indisputably the most celebrated and influential philosopher in the English-speaking world",[92] this imposing volume is the intellectual equivalent of being sexually assaulted by a unicorn: thrilling, terrifying, painful, wondrous, wholly unexpected and guaranteed to keep you awake at night.

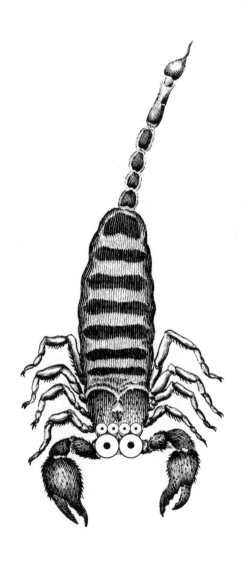

notes

1. Taken from *Principles of Social Reconstruction – Chapter V: Education* (Routledge, 1997) p.115.

2. T. S. Eliot's poem "Mr. Apollinax" presents an unforgettable portrait of Russell as, among other things, an "irresponsible foetus". First published in 1916 in both *Poetry* magazine, Chicago, and *The Egoist* magazine, London – thanks to the influence of Ezra Pound – and later included in T. S. Eliot's first anthology, *Prufrock and Other Observations*, published by The Egoist Ltd, London, in 1917 – thanks, once again, to the tireless Ezra Pound – Eliot's debut collection is credited with dragging Romantic poets into the Modernist age, kicking, screaming and utterly baffled.

3. Eliot, then a promising doctoral student in Harvard's prestigious philosophy department, first met Russell in the spring of 1914, when he attended Russell's guest lectures and also joined a gathering of twelve postgraduate students who had tea with Russell each week: Eliot was so impressed by Russell's distinctive voice and dazzling intellect he could not remember anything about any of his fellow attendees, other than that they ate cucumber sandwiches. Suffice to say Eliot greatly admired the distinguished visiting professor (acclaimed by fellow students as "almost superhuman" and by the eminent American philosopher, Josiah Royce, as "the most discussed logician since Aristotle"). Russell, in turn, thought very highly of the promising philosopher (and soon to be celebrated poet) who would go on to receive the Nobel Prize in Literature in 1948, two years before Russell himself.

After being awarded a scholarship to Merton College, Oxford, Eliot moved to England in the autumn of 1914, and a chance encounter with Russell on a London street resulted in a renewed and deeper friendship. When the presumed sexless Eliot joined Russell for dinner in London, in 1915, he surprised his host with his mysterious bride of two weeks, Vivienne Haigh-Wood: surprised and curiously aroused, it turned out. Russell promptly invited the financially strapped young couple to share his lodgings and soon seduced Mrs Eliot. Some scholars believe T. S. Eliot was complicit in his wife's extramarital affair – either way, this thoroughly toxic *ménage à trois* ably assisted the complete destruction of the fatally flawed Eliot marriage and no doubt contributed to Vivienne's cruel alienation, alleged drug abuse and mental breakdown. Eliot himself credited his failed first marriage and its aftermath with gifting him the state of mind necessary to create his most famous poem, *The Waste Land*.

4. Russell is the model for the pitilessly brilliant Sir Joshua Malleson in D. H. Lawrence's novel *Women in Love* (stormy sequel to *The Rainbow*; arguably his best work and also, tragically, the first of his novels to be banned and the only one to be seized and burnt by the authorities) and likely also Bertie Reid, the fractured man-mollusc in Lawrence's short story *The Blind Man*. You might imagine that two great men of letters, one central and the other peripheral to the Modernist movement – both hypersexual, slim-hipped, small-bodied, angry pacifists crowned with curiously distorted heads – would be the best of friends ... but in fact they did not enjoy an easy relationship; the irony was that D. H. Lawrence, oft persecuted as a literary libertine, considered Russell far too liberal. Strange but true.

5. Bertrand Russell directly inspired Mr Scogan, the cynically prescient character in Aldous Huxley's first novel, *Crome Yellow*, whose darkly astute observations presaged Huxley's most famous work, *Brave New World*.

6. As an interesting aside, Russell's seminal work, *The Scientific Outlook* (1931), appeared in print just one year before the publication of *Brave New World* (1932). Though Russell's publisher discouraged him from taking action against Huxley for plagiarism, it is generally accepted that Russell's book provided vitally important source material for Huxley's dystopian classic. Beyond their sometime friendship, this direct intellectual connection would explain, at least in part, why Russell was a vocal champion of *Brave New World* when many other leading scientific and literary figures, including H. G. Wells, the "father of science fiction" himself, considered Huxley's best-selling novel offensively bleak. Russell even made a knowing, though essentially positive, reference to the success of *Brave New World* in a prefatory note to the second edition of *The Scientific Outlook* (1949).

7. Aldous Huxley died on November 22nd, 1963, within the same hour as C. S. Lewis and President John F. Kennedy:

Huxley succumbed to laryngeal cancer on the wings of LSD, Lewis fell out of his sickbed to die in his brother's embrace, and JFK was shot repeatedly by Lee Harvey Oswald and/ or persons unknown while parading through the streets of Dallas, Texas. The perverse coincidence of this morbid timing bears no especial relevance to Bertrand Russell, or the subject of Active Idleness, but continues to shock and fascinate me nonetheless.

8. One cannot talk about Russell's extraordinary influence upon and within the realms of philosophy and logic without mentioning Ludwig Wittgenstein, and the reverse is also true. Wittgenstein was inspired to study the foundations of mathematics after reading Russell's *The Principles of Mathematics* (1903). They met rather suddenly in 1911, when Wittgenstein arrived in Cambridge to study under Russell and barrelled into the professor's rooms at Trinity College unannounced while Russell was taking tea with a learned colleague. Though initially unsure if the stormy Wittgenstein was mad, a genius, or both, Russell grew to love and admire his student, describing his brilliant pupil in the third volume of his autobiography as follows: "He was the most perfect example I have ever known of genius as traditionally conceived; passionate, profound, intense, and dominating."

9. Russell soon came to view Wittgenstein as his intellectual heir, and although this came to pass, insomuch as Wittgenstein went on to be regarded alongside Russell as the most influential philosophers of the 20th century, the two did not collaborate as Russell has hoped, and eventually they grew apart, largely on account of Wittgenstein's erratic behaviour and his growing belief that Russell, along with virtually every sentient being, could not hope to truly understand him or his work. Despite Wittgenstein's growing disdain for his former teacher, Russell generously wrote the introduction to *Tractatus Logico-Philosophicus*, explaining and thus affirming its importance: though less than eighty pages, this pugnacious little volume established Wittgenstein's professional reputation. In a cruel twist of fate it was Wittgenstein's harsh but accurate criticism of Russell's *Theory of Knowledge* that brought this major work to a shuddering halt. Deeply wounded by his protégé's cutting insights, Russell not only abandoned the 208-page manuscript in 1913 but, as revealed in a letter written in 1916 to his then lover (Lady Ottoline Morrell – a.k.a. "Lady Utterly Immoral", as she was nicknamed by Aldous Huxley), Russell also came to believe that he ". . . could not hope ever again to do fundamental work in philosophy".

10. Wittgenstein was born in Austria within a week of Adolf
    Hitler ... as were many other less well-known Austrians,
    I'm sure. Interestingly, however, these two historical figures
    attended the same provincial high school in Linz (K.u.k.
    Realschule) for at least part of the school year in 1904;
    however, they were never classmates – Hitler, who was a
    very poor student, was sent back a class, while Wittgenstein
    was promoted a year ahead of his peers – thus, despite their
    being the same age, the two youths were two full grades
    apart. Not being able to fathom what could possibly have
    transformed a sensitive boy into a demonic Nazi leader has
    led to desperate speculation that it might have been young
    Ludwig, the wealthy Jewish boy with evident intellectual
    superiority, who first seeded pathogenic anti-Semitism
    within the future German Führer's evil little heart; though
    no meaningful evidence exists to suggest that either of the
    two school boys even knew the other existed at the time.

11. Russell's pioneering work in mathematical logic proved
    a major departure point for the founder of computer
    science. The profound connection between these two great
    minds endures to this day at the Alan Turing Memorial,
    located next to the University of Manchester. The bronze
    plaque beneath the sombre statue of Turing holding an

apple features the following quote from Russell's essay *The Study Of Mathematics* (1902): "Mathematics, rightly viewed, possesses not only truth, but supreme beauty – a beauty cold and austere, like that of sculpture."

---

12. In *Paul McCartney: Many Years from Now*, written by Barry Miles (1998), and in numerous interviews, McCartney revealed that he sought out Russell in London in the mid 1960s, when the philosopher was living in nearby Chelsea. It was Russell who first told McCartney of the ominous conflict underway in Vietnam – which was, at that time, still largely unreported in the media – and who encouraged Paul to rouse his band's political conscience. McCartney then took Russell's message back to his fellow Beatles (who were recording a new album at Abbey Road Studios) where he claimed it had an immediate and lasting impact on the band, especially John Lennon. Indeed, Lennon later returned his MBE (Member of the British Empire, (awarded to each member of The Beatles by Queen Elizabeth II in 1965)), as a protest against Great Britain's support for American policy during the Vietnam War.

---

13. On the 14th of October, 1931, Albert Einstein wrote an unsolicited letter to Russell and it is abundantly clear from the gushy first paragraph (copied verbatim (in

English) below) that he was a genuine fan:

Dear Bertrand Russell

 For a long time I have had the wish to write you. All I wanted to do, was to express my feeling of high admiration of you. The clarity, sureness, and impartiality which you have brought to bear to the logical, philosophical and human problems dealt with in your books are unrivalled not only in our generation.

---

14. For what it's worth, Russell also appeared in the Bollywood film *Anan*, in 1967 – the man did it all.

---

15. Sadly these artworks are generally unsigned and thus remain uncredited, due to the anonymous and possibly oppressive workmanlike employment terms granted the artists by commercial printers in those eras. Modern copyright law can be traced back to the 15th century, perhaps earlier; however, such protections initially only applied to written works and the majority of the many "original" etchings I own, and that you'll find contained in this book, are almost certainly copies of copies of copies.

---

16. I have certainly done my best to present an accurate account throughout, though, as an academic, I promise only varying degrees of disappointment.

17. This self-serving paraphrasing is pilfered from Russell's introduction to the English-language edition of Wittgenstein's *Tractatus Logico-Philosophicus* (1922)

18. Beyond establishing a factual foundation, these endnotes are also intended to stimulate and amuse. If they also offend a certain class of person, well, that's probably all to the good.

19. Morris Raphael Cohen, then the Professor Emeritus of Philosophy at the College of the City of New York, was "an almost legendary figure in American philosophy, education, and the liberal tradition" and "a leader in American thought and life" according to the *New York Times* (January 31st, 1947).

20. Unlike Socrates, who was found guilty of similar charges, Russell did not seek solace in death, but in fact gleefully added this small-minded public rebuke to his growing list of honours – going so far as to include this glorious final line beneath his academic credentials published in the British edition of *An Inquiry into Meaning and Truth* (George Allen & Unwin, 1940): "Judicially pronounced unworthy to be Professor of Philosophy at the College of the City of New York."

21. From *Six Men* by Alistair Cooke (Knopf, 1977).

22. As realised by Sir John Tenniel in his timeless illustrations for Lewis Carroll's *Alice's Adventures in Wonderland*.

23. Specifically by Norbert Wiener, mathematical prodigy, inventor of cybernetics, MIT icon, and namesake of a large crater on the dark side of the moon, who was also, by many accounts, an enthusiastic public nose-picker.

24. This anecdote comes from Alistair Cooke's firsthand observations contained in his book *Six Men* (Knopf, 1977). Russell was especially fond of the Sherlock Holmes mysteries, and even made reference to the idiosyncratic

Baker Street detective in his work, including his glorious essay *The Conquest of Happiness* (1930).

25. The fact that in 1958 the Irish Modernist playwright and Nobel Laureate Samuel Beckett started driving the young André the Giant to school (because the praeternaturally large youth could not fit onto the Molien school bus) just reminds us how joyously and inexplicably strange the 20th century actually was.

26. And if not truly "one of a kind", then certainly far more rare than a sincere politician, the perfect pair of jeans and panda coitus.

27. Here I refer to, *Scuola di Atene*, one of the stunning Renaissance frescoes painted in the Vatican's Papal Palace by Raphael, between 1509 and 1511. This epic masterpiece, inspired by both Plato's *Academy* and Aristotle's *Lyceum*, is believed to contain a portrait of every major Greek philosopher.

28. Or rather, in terms of analytic philosophy, what we are thinking of when we think we are thinking of something.

29. This was a deeply unpopular undertaking as viewed

by mainstream America at that time, which further tainted Russell's already prickly reputation in the USA. However, for the record, though always wary of the Western superpower, Russell held genuine admiration and affection for America and Americans – he lived and worked in America for a number of years, two of his four wives were American, and he regarded the philosophy students at Harvard as far more receptive to new ideas than those he had encountered at Oxford, the Sorbonne and even his alma mater, Cambridge. Conversely, though it was often presumed by the American press that Russell's sympathy for socialist ideals made him a friend of the USSR, the philosopher in fact took a very dim view of Soviet policy, and was extremely critical of Russian anti-Semitism (taking the matter up directly with Nikita Khrushchev and letting the world know of his intense dissatisfaction with the Kremlin).

Largely taken from *Bertrand Russell's America: His Transatlantic Travels and Writings. Volume One 1896–1945*, by Barry Feinberg and Ronald Kasrils (Allen & Unwin, 1973).

---

30. In 1995 the Pugwash Conferences were jointly awarded the Nobel Peace Prize with Polish physicist Joseph Rotblat, who co-founded these distinguished gatherings with

Russell in 1957. Nobel Prizes are not, as a rule, awarded posthumously; however, had Russell been alive he would also have personally shared in this great honour, and it is therefore accepted that the 1995 Nobel Peace Prize is part of his enduring legacy.

31. Primarily from America's undereducated Christian Right, which, to any reasonable person, should be taken as a great compliment.

32. In his autobiography Russell recounts having read his parents' diaries and letters and, based on what he learned of these intimate strangers, it is evident he was far more impressed by his mother.

33. A belief no doubt inspired in part by the views of his (secular) godfather, John Stuart Mill, the esteemed philosopher who, with his wife, Harriet, wrote *The Subjection of Women* in 1861 (published in 1869).

34. In addition to campaigning and writing in support of women's rights, Russell ran for a seat in the House of Commons during the 1907 Wimbledon by-election as the first ever Suffragist candidate (representing the National Union of Women's Suffrage Societies): a bold act that

resulted in scorn and ridicule being heaped upon his defiant head, as well as a number of eggs being thrown (one of which hit Russell's wife in the face during a rowdy political rally at Raynes Park, in London). Though Russell's bid for office resulted in electoral failure it was a resounding success as a media event, helping to raise the profile of women's suffrage throughout the United Kingdom and the semi-civilised world (according to the Wimbledon Society's feature in the *Local Guardian*, 3 May 2013).

35. In *Six Men* (Knopf, 1977), Alistair Cooke shared Russell's own account of how, aged three or four, he fell out of his mother's carriage and bruised his penis. Later that day his kindly nurse gave the young boy careful instruction on how to soothe his swollen and tender organ in the bath on his own with a sponge. However, based on evidence readily available, such ministrations were clearly never going to prove sufficient.

36. An estimated 12,775 women in total, according to Peter Biskind's biography, *Star: The Life and Wild Times of Warren Beatty* (Simon & Schuster, 2010).

37. By which I mean Russell's first wife – Alys Pearsall Smith – who was some years older than her tormented

teenage admirer (Russell was barely seventeen when they first met) and therefore was not just a Quaker but an incredibly rare Quaker cougar!

38. The late Countess Russell (1900–1978).

39. This attributed quote is actually an elegant paraphrasing of Russell's frank view of common sense as expressed in a number of published lectures and articles, including *Our Knowledge of the External World as a Field for Scientific Method* (1914), *The Relation of Sense-Data to Physics* (1914) and the essay *Mind and Matter* (1925), which is also included in *Portraits from Memory and Other Essays* (1956).

40. A shortlist of highlights and lowlights from 1932 might include the following:

- Adolf Hitler formally became a German citizen in order to run for his adopted nation's highest office and, by mid-year, through cunning political manoeuvring and artful betrayal, he had positioned himself to be appointed Chancellor.

- The BBC World Service (then known as the BBC Empire Service) made its very first shortwave radio broadcast.

- Rebellions and revolutions were underway in Thailand (then Siam), Brazil, El Salvador and Chile.

- Japanese and Chinese forces fought the "Battle of Shanghai", and the "Chaco War" began between Bolivia and Paraguay.

- Japanese Prime Minister Tsuyoshi Inukai and French President Paul Doumer were both assassinated.

- Saudi Arabia became a unified kingdom under the rule of the House of Saud, and the Kingdom of Iraq came into being after being granted conditional independence from Great Britain.

- Norway claimed Greenland on the basis that a husky Norseman, namely "Eric the Red", established the first European colony there in 1000 CE.

- Bloody riots between Hindus and Muslims in Bombay resulted in thousands killed.

- America hosted both the Summer and Winter Olympic Games in the same year, joining France (and later Germany) as the only nations to do so.

- FDR became the US President and Arkansas Democrat Hattie Caraway became the first woman elected to the US Senate.

- Walt Disney released *Flowers and Trees*, the world's first full-colour film, to great critical and commercial acclaim, winning the first Academy Award for Best Animated Short Film.

- And finally, in a most unfortunate historical confluence, Ghandi undertook a six-day hunger strike in Pune's Yerwada Central Jail while millions of Russians were starving to death in the Soviet famine, just as the world's first Mars Bar rolled off the production line in Great Britain.

---

41. It is thanks to the *Principia Mathematica* that you and I can say, without doubt, that 1+1=2. After ten year's work, and in more than three hundred pages, Russell (and his friend and colleague, Alfred North Whitehead) delivered this fundamental proof to great academic acclaim. This monumental achievement ensured that we mere mortals can enjoy logical certainty as the foundation of basic arithmetic.

---

42. Speaking as an erudite layman with a deep interest in Russell's life and work, I would happily lodge an energetic hedgehog within my inter-gluteal cleft and smuggle this spiny wriggler across Europe on a unicycle rather than sit through a series of technical lectures on Mathematical

Logic or endure a working demonstration of Russell's seminal 1905 work *On Denoting*.

43. Specifically, semi-literate trust-fund rednecks.

44. Bear with me as we unravel an historical timeline as convoluted as a Möbius tapeworm. I'm speaking broadly about Russell's ultimate disappointment with the implementation of seemingly positive social, political and economic ideologies as viewed by the Great Man before, during and many years after he wrote this essay. In essence I'm condensing and simplifying Russell's hindsight from the future, so to speak. And finally, just so we are clear, the nationalist Republic of China did not give way to the communist People's Republic of China until the end of the Chinese Civil War in 1949 – twenty eight years after Russell last set foot in China and seventeen years after *In Praise of Idleness* was first published.

45. Russell used a great deal of his inherited capital to secretly pay off the considerable debts of his former teacher, friend and colleague Alfred North Whitehead OM FRS (from *Bertrand Russell*, by A. J. Ayer (1972)) and to establish The Beacon Hill School, a progressive elementary school, with his then wife, Dora Black. When

his brother died, Russell took custody of an earldom that was all but in hock, and he was therefore forced to earn a living by teaching and writing. Large popular works like *A History of Western Philosophy* provided his income for many years; he was, however, still obliged to give paid public lectures and write newspaper articles. From 1931 to 1935, for example, Russell contributed a weekly syndicated article to the Hearst Press. His need for money, however, was secondary to his indifference to celebrity and authority and so his fees got reduced, and then his articles were no longer welcome after Russell spurned an invitation to stay with William Randolph Hearst at his stately pleasure-dome in San Simeon, California. Hearst then had his hatchet men at the San Francisco *Examiner* savage Russell in a half-page illustrated feature within their popular Sunday edition that declared Russell an "enemy of the people" and an "admirer of sexual psychopaths". Curiously enough, it was this very article that piqued the interest of a talented tween named Wallace I. Matson (1921–2012), and ultimately led him to pursue philosophy as a career, culminating in Matson being appointed Emeritus Professor of Philosophy at the University of California, Berkeley, and featuring his legendary 1991 commencement address, entitled "The Study of Philosophy as a Prophylactic against Bullshit".

Largely taken from *Falling in Love with Wisdom: American Philosophers Talk about Their Calling* (Oxford University Press, 1993).

46. Here I owe an enormous debt to the fascinating insights offered in *The Organized Mind: Thinking Straight in the Age of Information Overload* (Dutton Adult, 2014), written by *New York Times* best-selling author and acclaimed neuroscientist Dr. Daniel J. Levitin.

47. According to *How Much Media? 2013 Report on American Consumers* (a study by the Institute for Communication Technology Management at the University of Southern California's Marshall School of Business) by 2015 the average American will consume 15.5 hours of media and 74 gigabytes of data every single day.

48. From *The Conquest of Happiness* (1930).

49. I did not know of this amusing and vaguely racist parable, nor have I found a second source to verify its provenance. Nevertheless it is quite true that, since late antiquity, Naples had been notorious for its horde of beggars that beset travellers as soon as they entered the city's gates; at least that is what British writers tell us (*The Spectator*, December 31st,

1864). However not all of Naples' homeless were beggars – most were merely desperately poor folk looking for odd jobs to survive; such as delivering messages or carrying luggage and goods for a small fee. During the Age of Revolution the Neapolitan homeless composed a considerable force (estimates range from 13,000 to as many as 50,000), and were known as the Lazzaroni. Far from an unruly mob, the Lazzaroni elected a chief from among their own every year and rose to fight when a cause suited them, as they did to help defeat the French in 1799 and thus bring Naples' short-lived Parthenopean Republic to a grisly end.

50. The modern reader may wonder why Russell chooses to make special mention of the YMCA almost fifty years before this noble institution inspired the the Village People to create the most beloved gay disco anthem of all time. The fact is that in 1932 the Young Men's Christian Association (now known simply as "The Y") was at the height of its cultural and political influence. Almost a century after being founded in London, in 1844, the YMCA was not only a haven for muscular Christians who sought safe housing and wholesome activities, but had become an influential evangelical and charitable body that wielded very real conservative political clout.

51. I'm not certain the purveyors of thirty-year fixed-rate Treasury Bonds would be pleased to know Russell compares their clients to Richard III and Macbeth.

52. By "surface cars" Russell is referring to what today are called streetcars, trolleys or trams. The advent of electric trams meant big business in the late 19th and early 20th century, hence his reference to this major industrial enterprise. One wonders though if Russell didn't have a special place in his heart for such a charming mode of public transportation, as the very first (horse-drawn) tramway originated in 1807 in Swansea, Wales, just seventy miles from where he was born.

53. The present British monarch's annual salary is roughly £40,000,000 British pounds (which, at the current exchange rate, is a shade over $85,000,000 Australian dollars). Though to be fair, Her Majesty, Queen Elizabeth II must cover all the expenses of the Royal Household, including the corgis.

54. Here Russell is referring to the First World War (1914–1918), known at that time as the Great War.

55. Russell's choice of a pin factory as his example seems to be an allusion to the famous and often misunderstood description of the almost limitless commercial potential derived from the modern division of labour as told by Adam Smith, "The Father of Economics", in his seminal work *An Inquiry into the Nature and Causes of the Wealth of Nations* (1776). Russell and Smith both shared many views typical of classical liberalism – but whereas Russell is so often condemned by bloated industrialists, the reluctant Smith is held aloft by Ayn Rand acolytes as the demigod of capitalism. As yet another curious aside: the Bank of England's £20 note was updated in March 2007 and today features a portrait of Adam Smith and an image of a pin factory.

56. The USSR existed from 1922 until its dissolution in 1991. Russell visited Russia in 1920, eager to see firsthand what positive changes had been wrought by the largely oppressive Tsarist autocracy being obliterated by the Bolshevik Revolution. He arrived in what was then the Russian Soviet Federative Socialist Republic, excited at the social potential of communism – however, he was appalled by the cruelty and deprivation he witnessed and left bitterly disappointed.

Taken largely from *The Practice and Theory of Bolshevism* (George Allen & Unwin, 1920).

57. After centuries of debate it was supposedly settled in British Parliament, in the early 1970s, that Monmouthshire was, is and shall forever be Welsh, though not everyone was convinced; hence, pained bleatings for a public referendum echo to this day.

58. Though undeniably the "black sheep" of the Russell dynasty, and something of a brute, Frank's wickedness *per se* is wildly overstated. All sexual and conjugal intrigue aside, the 2nd Earl Russell's boyish obsession with motorcars and his reckless depletion of the family estate brings to mind the profligate and rambunctious Mr Toad, of Toad Hall. In 1903 Frank queued outside the council offices all night in order to purchase the very first London number-plate, A1 – and in 1930, as Parliamentary Secretary to the Minister of Transport, he was instrumental in introducing the Highway Code and abolishing speed limits. Frank claimed to be a Buddhist and also to have a weak heart as the result of a traumatic divorce (though it is difficult to be certain as to which particular divorce he meant). I can't vouch for his devotion to the Noble Eightfold Path, but Frank might well have been right about his heart, for he died suddenly and without heirs, in 1931, at which time the Russell Earldom passed to his younger brother, Bertie.

59. Douglas Alexander Spalding initially studied law in Aberdeen and London, however just as he finished his degree he contracted tuberculosis. Not wanting to die a lawyer (and who can blame him?) Spalding became a self-taught biologist, and eventually achieved academic acclaim for his groundbreaking research into animal behaviour, especially with chickens. "The concepts of behavioral maturation and behavioral critical periods were invented by him ... [he was the first to recognise] the importance and interaction of both learned and instinctive behavior. He was the first to study the phenomenon which we now call imprinting ... [and] he was the first man to use the word *behavior* in its present psychological sense."

Taken from "Douglas Alexander Spalding: The First Experimental Behaviourist," by Philip Howard Gray (*The Journal of General Psychology*, Volume 67, Issue 2, 1962).

60. On May 25th, 1870, Lady Kate delivered a public lecture on *The Claims of Women* to a large audience in the elegant Subscription Rooms in Stroud. The crowd received her speech with polite applause at best, however afterwards impassioned letters poured into the *The Times* (then the most influential newspaper in the world), which caused a "considerable stir". Quivering with regal rage, Queen

Victoria dashed off a letter to the esteemed Scottish lawyer and poet Sir Theodore Martin, in which she condemned the "mad, wicked folly of 'Women's Rights'" and thundered that "Lady Amberley ought to get a good whipping".

From *The Women's Suffrage Movement: A Reference Guide 1866–1928*, by Elizabeth Crawford, Routledge, 2001.

---

61. Russell's mother and sister both died of diphtheria. The tragic twist is that they caught the disease from Russell's brother, Frank, who contracted it when he accompanied his parents (and Spalding) to Rome, where his father was hoping to recover his health following bouts of epileptic seizures. Little Rachel first showed symptoms once the family was reunited in Wales, mistakenly believing that Frank was cured of the disease following treatment in London. Lady Kate then contracted diphtheria while nursing her young daughter, and so the misery unfolded, with both mother and daughter dying five days apart. It is not surprising that, after burying his treasured daughter and cremating his beloved wife (which was considered a deeply un-Christian act by his peers), Lord John fell into a deep depression. His health deteriorated and he never recovered, dying of bronchitis eighteen months later (an eerily similar cause of death to his son, Bertrand, who succumbed to acute bronchitis ninety-five years hence).

Though by no means as charismatic (or nearly as popular) as Lady Kate, the bookish Lord John was considered quite brilliant and counted John Stuart Mill and George Santayana among his influential and learned friends.

Largely taken from *Betrand Russell: A Life*, by Caroline Moorehead (Sinclair-Stevenson, 1992) and the rather racy pages of *The Illustrated American* (Volume Nine, December 26th, 1891).

---

62. Young Bertie was a voracious reader – his treasured library represented both Russell's intellectual inheritance and also a lifeline, as evidenced by this quote from *Fact and Fiction* (1961), "From books I derived courage and hope and freedom in arduous endeavour."

---

63. Apart from possessing the most dashing set of whiskers since Sir Francis Drake, T. J. Cobden-Sanderson was also the person who gave the *Arts and Crafts* movement its name.

Largely taken from two feature articles about Cobden-Sanderson, "Book Binding and the Doves Bindery", by Emily Preston and Florence Foote in *The Craftsman Magazine* (Volume Two, Number One, April, 1902).

---

64. According to Russell, Pembroke Lodge was "a rambling house of only two storeys in Richmond Park. It was in

the gift of the Sovereign, and derives its name from the Lady Pembroke to whom George III was devoted in the days of his lunacy." George III suffered from debilitating mental illness during his long reign, on top of which he was the British monarch who lost America, so to speak. However, owing to the unique and often inexplicable British mindset, he remained an extremely popular king. The most enjoyable contemporary window into the life of George III, in my opinion, is the 1994 motion picture *The Madness of King George*, based on the superb play by Alan Bennett and starring the great Nigel Hawthorne (who sadly and, to my mind, unjustly, conceded the Oscar for Best Actor at the 67th Academy Awards to Tom Hanks for his titular role in *Forrest Gump*).

65. The "Bath chair" was a luxurious precursor to the modern wheelchair. A cross between a chaise longue on wheels and an oversized baby carriage, it allowed for the passenger to be pushed around by a person or, in some cases, drawn along by a pony or an especially ambitious goat. In his autobiography Russell admits to stealing his late grandfather's Bath chair and racing it down all the hills he could find, much to the horror of Lady Fanny and the household staff, who considered this a blasphemous act.

66. From *Bertrand Russell*, by A. J. Ayer (The University of Chicago Press, 1972)

67. Though fresh fruit is now considered essential to a healthy diet, especially for growing children, Lady Fanny's view was the exact opposite. In his autobiography Russell wrote that his grandmother held the unalterable Victorian conviction that fruit was bad for children – though why exactly is unclear. The difference between sucrose and fructose has been known for almost twenty years by the time Russell was born. Of course it's possible that Lady Fanny believed the consumption of anything sweet, like all forms of corporeal pleasure, might result in the damnation of her grandson's immortal soul. In any case Russell suffered little nutritional deprivation, as he conscientiously augmented his bland prescribed diet with stolen crabapples and blackberries from Pembroke Lodge's expansive gardens.

68. Russell's Uncle "Rollo" (Francis Albert Rollo Russell) was a distinguished natural science graduate from Oxford, who was elected to the Royal Meteorological Society at only nineteen. He may have gone on to do great things, but for his poor eyesight and his being, by nature, more timid than a soft-shelled crab who suddenly finds himself in the

middle of a Broadway stage during the board-thumping finale of *Riverdance*. Despite these handicaps, and his being forced to play the role of snivelling imp to his domineering mother, Lady Fanny, Rollo did undertake important scientific work and had a very positive influence over his nephew, Bertie. An avid and early environmental activist, Rollo's papers on London fog and smog were central to growing public demands for the reduction of coal-burning stoves to curtail increasingly toxic levels of air pollution. Rollo's chief claim to meteorological fame, however, was a paper titled "The Eruption of Krakatoa and Subsequent Phenomena", which he presented to the Royal Meteorological Society in 1883, just five months after the Indonesian volcano exploded with catastrophic consequences: the vast amount of airborne ash and dust particles spewed into the atmosphere affected weather patterns around the world and resulted in measurable global cooling for a period of almost five years. Rollo, working from home, let his eleven-year-old nephew assist him on this important paper, and in so doing instilled a love of science in Bertrand Russell that never left him.

69. Though the neglected gardens of Pembroke Lodge were Bertie's "Fortress of Solitude", the greatest revelation of his childhood was the moment when, aged eleven, young

Russell became acquainted with Euclidean geometry, thanks to his brother, Frank. Russell, in his autobiography, would describe his introduction to advanced mathematics as one of the great events of his life, going on to say that it felt "as dazzling as first love. I had not imagined there was anything so delicious in the world. From that moment until I was thirty-eight, mathematics was my chief interest and my chief source of happiness."

70. Though, to be fair, the Angry Birds of Bertie's day were, in fact, actual angry birds; most probably blackbirds and robins from whom he stole eggs for his childhood collection.

71. Largely taken from *The Oxford Handbook of Percy Bysshe Shelley*, edited by Michael O'Neill, Anthony Howe and Madeleine Callaghan (Oxford University Press, 2012).

72. A great deal is made of Russell's religious views (especially by groups vehemently expressing their desire to repudiate or claim the Great Man as one of their own), so I'll do my best to summarise these, and also provide some modern context: Russell was against absolute faith in any belief system (including scepticism). He stated many times that there was insufficient evidence to prove or disprove the

existence of God (by which he meant any and all "Gods"), therefore one had to suspend judgement until such irrefutable evidence was found. In the meantime he noted that God's existence, or nonexistence, did not unduly affect him. As such, Russell can best be described as an agnostic with apatheistic leanings. However, he would often describe himself as an atheist in less sophisticated company to simplify the issue and reduce the grounds for heated argument – much in the same way that the gifted British author Douglas Adams (of *The Hitchhiker's Guide to the Galaxy* fame) would describe himself as a "radical atheist" to avoid misunderstanding and irritating special pleading from religious friends and fans.

Though a humanist through and through, Russell took pains to present himself as a composed advocate for reason; he wished to be convinced, not converted, and allowed others the same courtesy. In *Sceptical Essays* (Allen & Unwin, 1928) Russell states "The opinions that are held with passion are always those for which no good ground exists; indeed the passion is the measure of the holder's lack of rational conviction." As far as Russell was concerned this applied equally to religious adherents and atheists. This being so, Russell's attitude and intellectual bearing places him at some distance from what has come to be known as New Atheism; the irony-free godless evangelical movement as championed by Richard Dawkins and his grandiloquent disciple Stephen Fry. And though their arguments are not without considerable merit I can't help but note that New Atheism seems to appeal most to very intelligent people who imagine themselves exceptionally intelligent.

While purely speculation, I suspect Russell would have enjoyed the connection between Dawkins' excellent work on chicken behaviour with that of his first tutor, Douglas Spalding, and no doubt would also have appreciated Dawkins' anti–Vietnam War stance while the latter was an assistant professor of zoology at U. C. Berkley in the late sixties. However, I wonder whether Russell might have taken a dim view of Dawkins' brand of atheism for at least two reasons: First, the emotive (if not downright caustic) tone that Dawkins and his followers favour – largely born of internet chat-room bravado – overshadows their substantive arguments and is often deliberately offensive and thus entirely unpersuasive. Just as supposed spiritual superiority results in sickening self-righteousness, so too atheist swagger results in unpalatable arrogance. Likewise an overreliance on condescension and mockery to goad an intellectual rival into public debate is both fruitless and in very poor taste. In this regard Dawkins fits the damning description Russell once applied to George Bernard Shaw: "He wanted to be witty at all costs and it led him into unbelievable cruelties." (from *Six Men*, by Alistair Cooke). Second, I can well imagine

Russell taking in Richard Dawkins' eponymous foundation, website and awards and observing, with exquisite dryness, that an excess of self-worship ultimately precludes one from actually being an atheist.

---

73. This scriptural sliver being the first part of Exodus 23:2.

---

74. An intelligent guesstimate found in *Bertrand Russell: The Spirit of Solitude 1872–1921*, by Ray Monk (Jonathan Cape, 1996).

---

75. Wantonly prolific throughout his life, Russell easily eclipses Agatha Christie in terms of number of published works (though not in terms of copies sold – while it may be hard to imagine, the public appetite for genteel murder mysteries far exceeds that of those clamouring for insights into Logical Atomism). In addition, the 40,000 Russell letters we know of (being only those letters kept safe within the Bertrand Russell Archives at McMaster University, in Ontario, Canada) represents millions more words than most authors will ever commit to ink.

By way of meaningless yet fascinating comparison, William Golding and John Steinbeck were among the few major authors to pen 3,000 words each day – and then only when neck deep in a novel. Stephen King and

P.G. Wodehouse both hover around 2,000, give or take. Hemingway wrote up to 1,000 words per day when the fish weren't biting, Graham Greene was happy at 500 words per day or even less, and Vladimir Nabokov, author of *Lolita*, wrote a mere 180 words per day – though to be fair Nabokov did spend the bulk of his working day examining the genitals of butterflies – no, not a nauseating euphemism, the gifted Russian émigré was a noted lepidopterist and his genital classification method has been proven to be one of the most sound ways to differentiate butterfly species.

Largely taken from *Odd Type Writers*, by Celia Blue Johnson (Perigee Books, 2013).

---

76. From *How I Write* (1954).

---

77. For the record: Russell always wrote by hand. I'm just trying to be clever.

---

78. Also from *How I Write* (1954).

---

79. From *A History Of Western Philosophy* (1945).

---

80. Unless of course, as many scholars now believe, Pythagoras didn't actually exist, in which case the term was obviously invented by someone else. Russell regarded Pythagoras,

the father of pure mathematics, as "intellectually, one of the most important men that ever lived. Both when he was wise and when he was unwise ... a combination of Einstein and Mrs Eddy." Mrs (Mary Baker) Eddy was the founder of the Christian Science movement, who was harshly ridiculed by Mark Twain in 1907. Therefore in the latter instance Russell is alluding to the eponymous religion Pythagoreanism, allegedly founded by Pythagoras (or perhaps just invented by a group of vegetarian Greek nutters who would not feel out of place in California). Among the many Pythagorean tenets are instructions not to walk on highways, to abstain from eating beans, and to never touch a white cock – all of which may well be good advice, depending on the situation.

Taken from *A History Of Western Philosophy* by Bertrand Russell (Allen & Unwin, 1945) and *The Book of Dead Philosophers* by Simon Critchley (2009, Vintage).

81. From *Sceptical Essays* (1928).

82. From *Is There a God?*, an essay written by Russell in 1952 but not published until it was included in *The Collected Papers of Bertrand Russell, Volume 11: Last Philosophical Testament, 1943–68*, John G. Slater and Peter Köllner (eds), (Routledge, 1997), Chapter 69, pp. 547–548.

83. From *The Problems of Philosophy* (1912) (Oxford University Press, 1959), Chapter 1, *Appearance and Reality* p. 7, and also Chapter 15, *The Value Of Philosophy* p. 161.

84. Russell contracted double pneumonia while in China, during the winter of 1921, and became gravely ill, hovering near death. During his treatment additional complications arose when Russell was also found to be suffering from heart disease, kidney disease, phlebitis and dysentery. After being nursed back to health by his future ex-wife, Dora Black, and an English nurse in a German hospital based in Beijing (then Peking), Russell was made aware of how near death he had been when he read copies of his obituary that had been written by Japanese journalists, as well as celebratory announcements published by Christian missionaries in China (weary of being made to look foolish by the revered scholar). With his cool wit, Russell made the following observation: "I was told that [had I died] the Chinese said that they would bury me by the Western Lake and build a shrine to my memory. I have some slight regret that this did not happen, as I might have become a god, which would have been very chic for an atheist."

In 1948 Russell, then in his mid seventies (roughly the same age as Socrates when he breathed his last), had a more dramatic brush with death while travelling from Oslo to Trondheim, when the flying boat he was aboard crash-landed into Hommelvika Bay and started to sink. In a twist of fate Russell's life was prolonged by smoking – insomuch that, when booking his passage, he had demanded a seat in the smoking section of the plane, joking that "If I cannot smoke [my pipe], I shall die". This lighthearted remark proved darkly prophetic, as only Russell and his fellow passengers seated in the rearward smoking section were able to escape the aircraft before it sank into the frigid depths of the Trondheimsfjord.

85. From Russell's obituary in the *New York Times* (February 3rd, 1970), by Alden Whitman.

86. From *Unarmed Victory* (1963).

87. From Russell's letter to Miss (Gladys) Rinder (July 30th, 1918), published in the second volume of Russell's *Autobiography*.

88. To quote Russell himself: "I am in no degree ashamed of having changed my opinions. What physicist who was active in 1900 would dream of boasting that his opinions had not changed?" From *The Bertrand Russell Dictionary of Mind, Matter and Morals* (1952).

89. From *What I Have Lived For*, written on July 25th, 1956 and included in Bertrand Russell's *Autobiography* (Routledge Classics, 2010) as the Prologue.

90. It is perhaps not surprising, but still heartwarming, to learn that Professor Noam Chomsky has, on his office wall at MIT, an extremely large poster of Russell that also features Russell's three defining life passions drawn from this very same quote. It's hard to imagine a better flag-bearer for Russell's values or a more valiant herald for the vital yet painful truths that all should know yet so few want to hear.

91. One colourful account of this game old bird is that, aged seventy-seven, Ayer faced down the world's most dangerous prize-fighter. According to the account published in *A.J. Ayer: A Life* by Ben Rogers (2002), Ayer was attending a party in 1987 at the swanky New York apartment of fashion designer Fernando Sánchez when he was summoned by a distraught young woman who claimed her girlfriend was being assaulted in the nearby bedroom. The petite Ayer, ever the gallant gentleman of letters (and a former secret agent), rushed to the lady's aid, his skinny legs ablur like a quail on a treadmill. When Ayer arrived he found the scene exactly as described,

but with two interesting additional details: First, the damsel in distress turned out to be the teenaged Naomi Campbell, soon to become a certified supermodel. Second, the alleged cad was none other than the fearsome Mike Tyson who, then in his thick-necked prime, had just become the undisputed heavyweight boxing champion of planet earth. Undaunted, Ayer demanded Tyson cease his carnal mauling, resulting in the following unforgettable exchange: "Tyson: 'Do you know who the fuck I am? I'm the heavyweight champion of the world.' Ayer stood his ground: 'And I am the former Wykeham Professor of Logic. We are both preeminent in our field; I suggest that we talk about this like rational men.' Ayer and Tyson began to talk. Naomi Campbell slipped out."

92. From "This Place is Hell: Bertrand Russell at Harvard", 1914, by Kirk Willis (*The New England Quarterly*, Volume 62, Number 1, March, 1989.)

93. The world's oldest and most prestigious scientific academy.

BERTRAND ARTHUR WILLIAM "Bertie" RUSSELL, 3rd Earl Russell, OM FRS, was a British mathematician, philosopher, logician, historian and writer. Born in Trellech, Monmouthshire, Wales, in 1872, Russell was raised by his grandmother at Pembroke Lodge, in London. As a boy Russell showed remarkable academic ability when first exposed to the principles of Euclidean geometry and went on to win a mathematics scholarship to Trinity College, Cambridge. After graduating with distinction he went on to produce an extraordinary volume of ground-breaking work in his field and was elected a Fellow of the Royal Society[93] in 1908, aged only thirty-five, and received the Order of Merit from King George VI in 1949. Regarded as one of the most luminous minds in the history of humanity, Russell received the inaugural Butler Gold Medal, for his distinguished contribution to philosophy, in 1915; the De Morgan Medal and the Sylvester Medal, for his outstanding contributions to mathematics, in 1932 and 1934 respectively; and the Nobel Prize in Literature, in 1950. In addition to his exceptional academic standing Russell was a man of the people, and in 1957 he received the Kalinga Prize from the United Nations Educational, Scientific and Cultural Organization (UNESCO) for his outstanding contribution to the interpretation of science and technology to the general public. Russell was also a tireless social critic, a fearless political activist and a dauntless champion for peace, justice and equality who was twice imprisoned for his views. He launched the Bertrand Russell Peace Foundation in 1963, and was awarded the inaugural Jerusalem Prize in that same year. He also established the International War Crimes Tribunal in 1967. Lord Russell died of influenza at *Plas Penrhyn*, his home in Penrhyndeudraeth, Wales, on February 2nd, 1970.

BRADLEY TREVOR GREIVE, AM, was born in Hobart, Tasmania, in 1970, twenty days after Lord Russell's death. BTG lived abroad with his family for most of his childhood, in Scotland, Wales, England, Hong Kong and Singapore, before returning to Australia to complete his education. After graduating from the Royal Military College, Duntroon, BTG served as a Paratrooper Platoon Commander in the Australian Army. Upon leaving the military he began a career in publishing as a cartoonist with the *Sydney Morning Herald* and has since gone on to become one of the world's most successful humour authors, with global sales now in excess of 25,000,000 copies across 115 countries. A semi-indestructible adventure sportsman, certified cosmonaut and a Polynesian rock-lifting champion, BTG is also a wildlife expert and television personality. His reputation as a serious literary figure has been somewhat compromised by his being attacked by woolly monkeys, porcupines, reindeer and fairy penguins; on at least one occasion he was sexually assaulted by a giant bat and has so far endured five treatments for rabies. BTG was awarded the Order of Australia in 2014 for his services to literature and wildlife conservation. BTG is married and currently divides his time between Australia and the USA in order to placate his American in-laws.

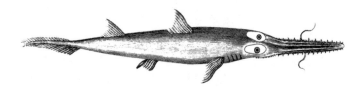

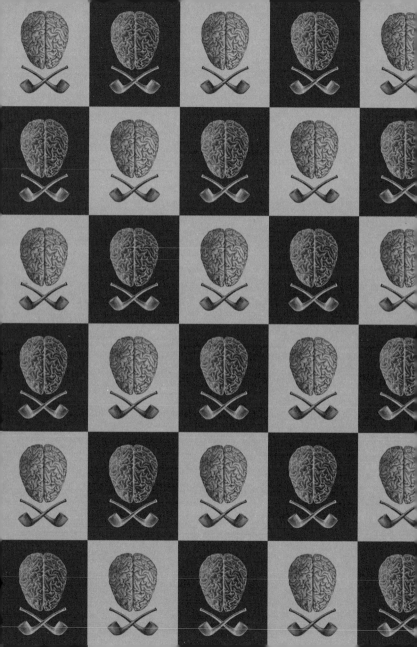